SUCCESS

Redefined

A new era
of empowerment

Keelan,
Align your heart with
your head & you'll
always succeed,
Love you to bits,
Karen

THE MONARCH & CO.

Success Redefined

The Monarch & Co.
www.themonarchandco.com
Contact at info@themonarchandco.com

EDITING: The Monarch & Co. Publishing Team, with Lead Editor Christine Stock

COVER & INTERIOR DESIGN: Michelle Fairbanks

ISBN SOFTCOVER: 978-1-0692183-5-3
ISBN EBOOK: 978-1-0692183-6-0

SUCCESS

Redefined

A new era
of empowerment

AMANDA WILSON-CIOCCI | NADIA PEZZIN | EMILY RAND
AMY SUSSEX | ASHLEE LIVINGSTONE | ANDREA KRONES
CATHERINE FARQUHARSON | NINA RUELENS
KAREN ARMSTRONG | BRITTANY MILLER | LAURA SINCLAIR

CONTENTS

AN INVITATION FOR YOU . . .

Have you ever been driving a vehicle, then thought after arriving at the destination, *How the heck did I get here?*

You are completely capable and conscious. You have accelerated and braked when necessary. You've indicated turns and maybe even smiled at those on the commute. You are conscious of the actions you're making, but really, you're on autopilot—going through the motions, following the posted signs, heading toward the destination, and hoping you arrive at the place you intended when you set out at the start of the journey.

But is this destination the one *you* really want?

One year before this book came into existence, I was dreaming about how I wanted it to take form. I started writing out the idea of where it came from, who would write in it, and why it was important.

My name is Amanda Wilson-Ciocci, and I'm the owner of The Monarch & Co. For more than twenty years, I've helped visionary entrepreneurs build, grow, and launch their dream businesses with clarity, confidence, and love. Two years ago, my husband, Kiel, officially joined the company, and we launched the legacy arm of The Monarch & Co.: our boutique publishing house. Now, we have the honour of publishing books that create positive ripple effects for readers and a legacy for authors.

I dreamed of this book being a way to disrupt what is happening in our landscape: entrepreneurs following outdated scripts and models, driving themselves out of alignment and into burnout, feeling the chaos of rapid change and the effects of AI, and wondering where their place is by questioning what they *should do* versus what they are designed and lit up to do.

When I extended the initial invitation to write in this book, I said it was about rewriting the rules and creating new paradigms for success that align with our values, purpose, and vision for the future. That this would be an opportunity to disrupt old ways of thinking and be part of a movement that is shifting the landscape for entrepreneurs.

But along the way, I found myself getting stuck. I started creating rules without knowing it. I thought that in order to write for this book, someone would need to be X years in business, have X years of experience, and be generating a certain level of revenue. I started creating checkboxes and criteria. I started creating the very definition of success I was trying to disrupt, long before I'd even written a single word or read a single author application.

That's how deeply these ideas are wired into us.

Our definition of success is largely socially constructed and neurologically reinforced rather than individually chosen. From a young age, we're taught that success is money, title, recognition. And that doesn't just come from our families. It comes from school systems, family expectations, media narratives, and workplace structures. These beliefs are so unconscious, we think they're ours.

When I realized what I was doing, I stopped and asked myself: *Who am I to redefine success? Who are any of us? Are we reinforcing the norms that we don't even know are present? Or is there something deeper that deserves the mic here?*

These questions led me to throw out my checkboxes and criteria entirely. And what I found on the other side of that was gratitude: gratitude for seeing with a new lens and a much better book.

Most of us inherit our definitions of success. We perform these definitions until something breaks. Maybe a signal arrives or we turn inward or let go, but ultimately, it's not until we choose to listen, to see with new eyes, and to wake up to the choices we've been making and why we make them.

This book isn't here to hand you a new definition for an outdated term. It's here as an invitation. A place to land, read, and reflect on your own life so that you can ask the right questions and consciously create your own definition.

In a world flooded with generated content, the human story is what people desire to connect to. And it is precisely that truth, transferred from lived experience to the pages in your hands, that creates the kind of ripple effect in which we are honoured to be a part.

Our hope in sharing our stories is that it gives you permission to live yours. To borrow the courage, tune into that inner knowing, listen to the voice that whispers (or sometimes shouts) that there's a different way. One that's truer, more aligned, and *more you.*

Everything you need is within you. Let this book shine a light in those places within. Let it ask the right questions so you can make sure you're driving on the right path, in the right car, and listening to the track that sparks joy instead of keeping you numb. The goal isn't to arrive at your destination capable and conscious, it's to enjoy the journey and light it up along the way!

One

AMANDA WILSON-CIOCCI

DEDICATION

This book is dedicated to my family—Kiel, Koen, Giulia, and Luca. You are the loves of my life and the reason I believe so wholeheartedly in building a life and business that creates a positive ripple effect.

To the extraordinary co-authors of *Success Redefined*, thank you for your courage to show up honestly and share your truth. Every chapter is proof that when we dare to live, lead, and speak from the heart, our stories have the power to transform.

And to the Monarch community, the entrepreneurs, leaders, and dreamers rising together every day, you are the momentum behind this movement. Your dedication to growth, to impact, and to doing business differently reminds me of why this work matters so much.

This book is a celebration of what becomes possible when bold voices come together and dare to redefine success on their own terms.

AMANDA WILSON-CIOCCI

Amanda Wilson-Ciocci is the founder of The Monarch & Co.—an entrepreneurial ecosystem built for heart-centred leaders who are ready to build momentum, deepen their impact, and create a legacy that lasts.

Amanda is the creator of Monarch Momentum, a business accelerator and mastermind community for visionary entrepreneurs, as well as the founder of The Monarch & Co. Publishing House, where she guides authors through the transformative process of turning their message into a book.

With more than twenty years' experience as a business strategist, and a two-time best-selling author herself, Amanda is known for helping entrepreneurs get clear on their message, simplify what's overcomplicating their business, and step into their next chapter with confidence and purpose.

When she's not mentoring entrepreneurs or releasing books into the world, you'll likely find Amanda by the water with her family in Ontario, cooking something beautiful, or dreaming up the next ripple of impact.

Connect with Amanda on Instagram
@themonarchandco or visit **www.themonarchandco.com**

THE ARRIVAL FALLACY

Have you heard of the arrival fallacy?

The person who first coined this term was Dr. Tal Ben-Shahar (a Harvard professor) in his 2021 book *Happier, No Matter What: Cultivating Hope, Resilience, and Purpose in Hard Times.* The arrival fallacy is the idea, albeit a false one, that when you reach a goal, you will have an overwhelming feeling of contentment for having "arrived" at that destination. It's a seductive idea that most of us have been living inside of for a long time.

Consider Heinrich Böll's parable of the fisherman:

A Harvard MBA banker visiting a small Mexican village noticed a fisherman who'd returned early with a fine catch. When asked why he didn't stay out longer, the fisherman shrugged. He had enough. He spent his days sleeping in, fishing a little, playing with his children, taking siestas with his wife, and strumming guitar with friends in the evenings. "I have a full and busy life," he said.

The banker saw an opportunity. He laid out a fifteen- to twenty-year plan: bigger boat, then a fleet, then a cannery, then an IPO; millions in the bank. "And then what?" the fisherman asked. The banker smiled: "Then you retire, sleep late, fish a little, play with your kids, take siestas with your wife, and spend evenings in the village sipping wine with your friends."

The banker embodies the arrival fallacy. His entire pitch is built on the assumption that the fisherman needs to *arrive* somewhere before he can enjoy the life he already has. The banker is chasing a destination, believing fulfillment lives at the end of a twenty-year road. The fisherman exposes the fallacy. He never bought into the idea that satisfaction was waiting somewhere ahead. He's not striving toward a future version of his life, he's *living* it now.

Many of us find ourselves in the banker's shoes, grinding toward a finish line that keeps moving, and we don't even know it. The fisherman demonstrates what life looks like when you stop waiting to arrive.

In 2021, our realtor called and said, "It's time to move." We weren't looking to move. We loved our little three-bedroom home with a bunkie office in the backyard and a street named after a tree. After declining twice to see the other home, the third time was apparently the charm.

I went to see the six-bedroom home with a one-bedroom apartment and fell in love with the potential. Our realtor said that with the housing market the way it was, it would be a sideways, or lateral, move, meaning we could upgrade to a larger home without increasing our current mortgage. While I loved our little home, the thought of more space and an office I didn't have to "commute" to in the winter was intriguing.

That afternoon, I was on my yoga mat when one of my favourite quotes by Guriji B.K.S. Iyengar guided my thoughts and actions: "Do not think of yourself as a small, compressed, suffering thing. Think of yourself as graceful and expanding, no matter how unlikely it may seem at the time."

I called our realtor and said, "If you can make this move sideways, then we'll sell it!"

Two weeks later, we listed and sold.

In March 2021, we moved into that six-bedroom home and expanded in every way.

The Monarch & Co. grew some serious wings and took flight; we continued launching our signature program (Monarch Business Academy), the digital marketing agency was growing a roster of devoted happy clients, I wrote and published my first best-selling book (*The Monarch*), and we launched Monarch Momentum (a business community for heart-centred entrepreneurs). We also renovated the attached apartment and turned it into a beautiful bed-and-breakfast.

On the personal side of things, we bought our dream Jeep, adopted a dog, and began homeschooling our three kids through a rapidly changing landscape and global pandemic.

We were ticking *all the boxes*, but something wasn't right. We had built exactly what we said we wanted—the business, the home, the growth, the recognition—and still, there was a quiet but persistent gap between what we had and how we felt. The gap was the arrival fallacy. It's not loud and obvious, it just hums underneath the surface, growing louder the more boxes you tick.

The changing landscape was creating pressure on us we weren't consciously aware of. Then, in November 2022, we were surfing Netflix and landed on a 2021 documentary directed by Matt D'Avella called *The Minimalists: Less Is Now*, and something shifted. It's a film that demonstrates the benefits of living according to minimalism. It ends with a challenge: remove one item on day one, two on day two, three on day three, all the way to day thirty. We were up for the challenge!

Together, we each did this: Kiel, me, and our three kiddos (ages twelve, nine, and five at the time). To our surprise, the kids loved it! Each day they were excited to go through items they could remove, sell, or donate. What started as a fun family challenge became an opportunity for awareness, beautiful conversations, and deeper questions:

- What is truly important to our family?
- How much do we need to be happy?
- Is our life unnecessarily complicated or busy?
- What do we value?
- How do we define success?

As the film states: "Minimalism is the thing that gets us past the things, so we can make room for life's most important things, which actually aren't things at all."

We looked around at our new large home. Three of the six bedrooms weren't being used. I'm a big fan of feng shui, and the fact that we had so many "dead zones" in our home was not something I enjoyed. Plus the more than four hours each week to clean them! On top of that, the gap between the dream and reality of running a bed-and-breakfast in our home was starting to grow wider. Middle-of-the-night fire alarms, calls to unclog the toilet, and weekend guests with loud tunes while we put kids to bed were not exactly what we envisioned when we created this space.

On Day 7 of the Minimalist Challenge, we called our realtor and said, "It's time to move!" And just six months later, we moved to a three-bedroom home by the water.

Before I tell you what came next, I want to tell you about something that happened when I was twenty-two years old: I was diagnosed with cancer.

I share this part of my story because it gave me something most people don't receive until much later in life—the understanding that time is your most precious resource. That gift, as terrifying as it was to receive at such a young age, has shaped every meaningful decision I've made since. It's why the next exercise matters so much to me.

Have you ever measured your life? Not in an external net worth or collection of achievements kind of way, but in time?

Shortly after moving to our home by the water, Kiel and I did what we now call the Tape Measure Exercise. Here's how to do it: Grab a large sheet of paper (chart paper works best!). Using a tape measure, draw a simple line and mark your current age, your children's ages, and your parents' ages.

Something shifts when you see your life laid out in actual space. It stops being abstract. The years your kids are still home, the time you have left with aging parents (based on average life expectancies), the window you have for your own dreams—it all becomes visible and real.

From there, sit with these eight areas and let the questions guide you:

SEASON OF LIFE: What matters most right now, and what can wait?

CHILDREN AND FAMILY: How much time do you actually have left in this stage, and how do you want to use it?

AGING AND ELDERS: What conversations, memories, or moments need to be prioritized now?

YOUR DREAMS: Which ones feel time-sensitive, and which ones have been waiting for you to action?

ENERGY AND HEALTH: What rhythms would support the life you actually want?

WORK AND PURPOSE: What would right-sized success look and feel like in this season?

PRESENCE AND LEGACY: Zooming out to the whole timeline, what actually matters most?

PRACTICAL GROUNDING: What needs a yes? What deserves a loving no?

Close by finishing these four sentences:

1. If this season had a theme, it would be . . .
2. One thing I want to honour more deeply is . . .
3. A shift I'm ready to make now is . . .
4. Ten years from now, I'll be grateful I chose to . . .

This exercise won't give you a five-year plan, it gives you something more valuable. **The Tape Measure Exercise gives you clarity about the season you're in so the choices you make today are ones you'll still feel good about when you look back at this line.** This exercise makes you the conscious driver: awake, aligned, and intentional.

The Tape Measure Exercise didn't just show us what we valued personally, it asked us to look honestly at the work we were doing, the impact we were making, who we were helping, and more importantly, why.

I've always been fascinated by stories. As a kid, I would sit at the table and ask the adults around it to share parts of their life: the "why" behind their decisions, what motivated their choices, and the stories that put colour between the lines. I remember a family gathering when one of my older cousins, clearly annoyed by my long list of questions, asked, "Why do you ask so many questions? Why do you care so much?" I replied, "I just do." I was seventeen years old and could spend hours in deep conversations, learning the why behind the what. As it turns out, this thread of passion has followed me my whole life.

Stories are threads that connect us, the words that inspire us, the thoughts that challenge us. A single chapter can inspire a decision, and a question can change the course of a life. You can probably think of a book, a story, or a quote that has, in some way, changed or shaped who you are today. That is impact and legacy. And that is the work I want to create, support, and publish.

The Monarch & Co. Publishing House is our answer to the Tape Measure Exercise. It's the work we'll look back on and know matters in this season. Writing a book will crack you open in ways you cannot possibly prepare for. It is the journey of finding clarity in your voice, and it is the heart behind your mission. Helping entrepreneurs share and publish their stories is what we are here to do, and we are honoured to do it. I will continue to hold and weave with this thread that has followed me throughout my life.

Since childhood, we are taught to believe that external "things" will create the success we seek. You'll hear it in the "when/then" trap, when we make statements like "When I get X, then I'll be happy." As Ben-Shahar reminds us, money enables a wealthy life, but what truly defines success is not the external measures we seek but everything else.

Our wealthy life was not in the things. We moved from a six-bedroom home to a three-bedroom home by the water. We downsized, simplified, and let go of the bed-and-breakfast, the empty rooms, and the pressure to keep ticking boxes.

And we gained everything that actually matters. Our home has a private beach. There are no dead zones, no stranger's clogged toilets, no lists to check off. Instead, there are nightly dinners together, slow mornings, deep conversations, and lots of laughter and love. **We don't fill our space with things, we fill our time with joy.**

We live like the fisherman: sleeping in for slow mornings, playing with the kids at the beach, and doing work that is meaningful and fulfilling. And we didn't do it by arriving after twenty years of grinding for something we already had. We did it by choosing, again and again, to be exactly where we are.

From the outside, it might not make sense. But it never had to. Happiness is an inside job, wealth is what you create, and success? **Success is what you define it to be. It's the courage to keep driving toward what's actually yours; awake, aligned, and intentional.**

Two

NADIA PEZZIN

DEDICATION

To the parts of me that learned the hard way that endurance is not the same as strength.

To the version of me that chooses alignment over approval.

To those I love who have walked beside me through every version of my becoming.

To my partner, Rick, for believing in me and for standing beside me through this journey.

Lastly, to Amanda and Brandon. Being your mom is one of my greatest honours in this lifetime. I am so proud of you. Love you to the moon and back, and back again . . .

NADIA PEZZIN

Nadia Pezzin spent much of her life believing endurance was strength and that her worth was measured by how much she could carry without breaking. After losing her eyesight at nineteen, navigating marriage and motherhood in her twenties, leaving a life that looked perfect from the outside, surviving abusive dynamics, and ultimately experiencing burnout, she reached a point when pushing through was no longer possible.

Stepping away from a successful career with no clear plan forced her to confront who she was without performance, productivity, or approval.

Today, she is the founder of NP Promotions, where she helps companies lead with integrity through intentional branding and product strategy. Her work reflects the same values she fought to reclaim in her personal life: alignment, authenticity, and courage.

Nadia writes and speaks about learning to listen to yourself before burnout forces you to, redefining success beyond output, and building a life and business rooted in truth rather than expectation. She is still unlearning and still growing, and she is deeply committed to living from alignment instead of obligation.

Connect with Nadia on Instagram
@bynadiapezzin or visit **www.nppromo.ca**

THE MOMENT I LISTENED

It wasn't always like this. I didn't grow up asking myself what success meant to me. No one ever sat me down and said, "Define this for yourself." Instead, I absorbed it. I watched. I learned by observation. I paid attention to what was praised, what was rewarded, what made adults nod in approval.

Being helpful made you good.
Being capable made you safe.
Being agreeable made you lovable.
Rest required justification.
Carrying more made you valuable.

For most of my life, success looked like endurance. It looked like pushing through fatigue, like staying quiet when something felt wrong, like smiling when I wanted to scream, and like showing up even when I was unravelling inside. But endurance is not the same as strength.

From a young age, I noticed patterns. Teachers awarded diligence over curiosity. People were praised for not complaining, for being mature, for handling it well. Obligation was framed as responsibility, and compliance and endurance were framed as character. I internalized this message: strong people endure, anything else is weakness. This is where survival became my metric and my compass.

I measured my worth by how much I could survive without breaking. If I was overwhelmed but still performing, I was winning. If I was exhausted but still delivering, I was valuable. If I was hurting and no one could tell, I was strong. Being honest felt dangerous. Being tired felt weak. Having needs felt selfish. So, I learned to override them and not listen.

This definition followed me into adulthood. It shaped the relationships I entered, the roles I took on, and the standards I held myself to. I said yes more often than I paused. I volunteered, overdelivered, arrived early, and stayed late. I was the one people could rely on. The strong, stable, capable one.

Emotions and vulnerability were for the weak, and I was always okay because I was strong and could endure. I recall abusive relationships and situations where I didn't choose myself because I didn't want to make anyone uncomfortable. I didn't want to "cause trouble" and be the difficult one. I didn't want to disrupt the peace, even though when I look back, I can see that peace was costing me my own. So, I carried on and told myself I was being patient. I told myself I was being forgiving and that love required sacrifice. But what I was really doing was abandoning myself quietly, one moment at a time.

What I would clearly say to my younger self today is: **Forgiveness is internal and access is external.** If something harms you, emotionally, physically, mentally, the first step isn't forgiveness, it's choosing yourself. **Healing is always better than hiding. You do not earn love by enduring harm, and you do not prove your worth by absorbing someone else's dysfunction. We cannot fix the world while we tolerate what breaks us.** But I didn't know that then.

At nineteen years old, I lost my eyesight. There is something about losing a sense that sharpens your emotional survival. I adapted; I compensated. I had two successful corneal transplants over two years and proved to myself and everyone else that I could handle life. At twenty-two, I was married. At twenty-eight, I had two children. By thirty, I was divorced, grieving my father, raising my young kids, and holding a mortgage in my own name.

I remember standing in my kitchen late one night when my kids were asleep. The house was finally quiet and I was staring at my to-do list. The only sound was the hum of the refrigerator. My body felt like it weighed a thousand pounds, and my mind would not turn off. *You chose this. You left. You deserve this unease because you chose to leave!* I was shamed for leaving what looked like a successful life: a beautiful home, a husband who provided, a sense of stability. *What more could I want?*

Approval is never a reliable compass. When you measure your worth by what others expect, you give away your power. Success is rooted in your own values, not their applause.

What I didn't share was that the life I was living never truly felt like mine. I was on stage in someone else's play, performing a role that looked right to the audience but felt misaligned in my body and soul. After the divorce, my survival mode intensified. I purchased a home for my children and me. I returned to work full time and took on the role of provider. I was good at it. Over-functioning became my specialty. I could anticipate needs before they were voiced. I could manage crises. I could juggle responsibilities. Being needed was where I built my worth, and the more I could carry, the more valuable I felt.

I carried the guilt of disrupting our family unit for more than a decade. It lived in my thoughts. *Why couldn't I just stay? Why couldn't I just make it work? Why did I change everything*? I felt being responsible for all of it felt noble. Strong. Necessary. I would soon learn that this isn't sustainable, and the perfect storm was brewing inside of me.

In 2020, when the world shifted, something inside me began to shift too. On paper, I had a successful career. I was the go-to person for problems others avoided. I worked long hours, and my salary supported the lifestyle I had labelled as success. The house.

The security. The comfort. It worked until it didn't. When the pandemic forced everyone home, I found myself leaving for work while my children tried navigating logging into virtual school. I remember getting in my car and hearing conflicting whispers: *They need you. But I need to get to the office; I will be home soon*. I could so deeply feel the split in me. Yes, I was making money, but could I justify how I was feeling? Was this what I was working so hard for only to miss the very life I was building? This question lingered . . .

Burnout doesn't arrive dramatically; it whispers first. I became irritable over minor issues. A spilled cup of coffee felt like a catastrophe, an email felt like overwhelm. I had headaches that sent me into dark rooms, lying down to try and quiet the pounding behind my eyes. Wine became a nightly ritual—not for celebration, but for relief. I scrolled mindlessly, numbing the low hum of dissatisfaction I couldn't quite name. My calendar was packed, by me, and yet I resented it at the same time. Burnout is the finish line of a race we sign up for daily.

Before burnout, there were flags:

- Irritability
- Numbing
- Resentment
- Overcommitment
- Exhaustion that sleep does not fix

What I learned through my own burnout is that listening to yourself does not mean waiting until your body, or someone else, hands you a clear action plan. It means noticing that you are in discomfort and pausing long enough to ask why.

One afternoon, I had another headache. I closed my office door and turned off the lights. My mind said: *Push through*. My body said: *Stop*. A quieter voice whispered: *Maybe you need to work less?*

But I thought, *If I work less, I will disappoint my team. I won't be seen as capable. I'll be seen as failing.*

Listening felt selfish and irresponsible. It felt like betrayal. This was the beginning of me reclaiming my voice. By February 2021, I could no longer ignore or override the signs. I took a sick leave. The moment I said this out loud and sent the email, my chest tightened, my hand shook, I felt shame, and I felt exposed. *If I'm not needed, who am I? If I'm not performing, what is my value?*

I didn't share the news of my sick leave with many people. I felt like I had failed some invisible test of endurance. For years, I believed sick leave was for weak people who couldn't handle pressure, and I prided myself on handling pressure. **But burnout wasn't a failure of strength, it was a signal that I had lost the ability to choose.** When you are burned out, you are on autopilot. You put out the next fire, you survive the day, and your nervous system is in constant fight or flight. There is no room for creativity or vision or joy. Only reaction and doing.

For most of life, I treated my symptoms with bandages instead of looking at the actual wounds. Tired? Coffee. Overwhelmed? Work harder. Disconnected? Wine. Unfulfilled? Earn more. Unhappy? Upgrade something external. Quick fixes were easier than treating the wounds. That required uncomfortable honesty: *Why do I believe my worth is tied to output? Why do I tolerate environments that benefit from my depletion? Why do I feel responsible for everyone else's comfort but my own?*

It was a hard truth to realize I wasn't just enduring exhausting systems, I was participating in them. I said yes, overextended myself, and equated being needed with being loved. I had confused endurance with virtue. True strength is not silent suffering. True strength is self-confrontation. **Endurance as self-abandonment**

erodes you. Endurance as growth refines you. The difference is alignment.

In June 2021, with my hand on my heart, I handed in my resignation. No backup plan. No certainty. Just trust that I could no longer build a life that felt misaligned. People were disappointed. Some questioned my decision and felt it was risky. Some implied I was ungrateful. I had to learn to tolerate being misunderstood, to tolerate inconvenience, to tolerate others defining my story. **I learned that the real failure was not in disappointing others but in abandoning myself.**

For years, I surrounded myself with needy people who benefited from my over-functioning. But what I have learned is that there are different kinds of people. There are caring ones who will say, "Go home. You look exhausted. You don't have to prove anything."

When your environment constantly devalues you, whether it's subtle or not, it's not a challenge to work harder. This is a whisper worth listening to. You cannot redefine success in an environment that rewards self-abandonment. I used to believe success lived in the output. Now I know it lives in alignment. Success is the relationship I have with myself when no one is watching. It is listening when my body says to slow down. It is choosing presence over performance. It is saying no without apology. It is building from passion and heart rather than pressure.

Some days, success looks like leading and earning. Other days, it looks like drinking coffee in my favourite mug and relaxing on the deck with my dogs at my feet and nowhere to rush off to. I can remember being away at a conference, surrounded by a room full of ambition and achievement, and thinking, *I can't wait to be home. To sit on my deck. To drink my coffee slowly . . . and breathe.* That simple image felt more successful than anything in that room. Success is not me trying to avoid failure. It is refusing to give up on myself. It is failing in ways that protect your peace instead of your image. It is understanding that rest is strategic not indulgent.

Looking back, there wasn't one dramatic turning point; instead, there were many small moments. The headache I didn't ignore. The no I finally said. The resignation letter I handed in. The quiet morning coffee I savoured without guilt. Listening didn't arrive as clarity, it arrived as courage. Courage to pause, to disappoint, to leave, to redefine. I began listening, and everything began to change—not instantly, not perfectly, but with honesty and alignment.

If I were to share what this journey required, it would look something like this:

1. Notice the whispers before they become breakdowns.
2. Treat irritability, numbing, and resentment as signals—not personality flaws.
3. Pause long enough for your nervous system to breathe.
4. Question the belief that your value is tied to output.
5. Leave what harms you. Forgiveness does not require access.
6. Surround yourself with people who want you well, not just useful.
7. Accept that you will disappoint people.
8. Define success in a way that feels aligned in your body.
9. Make small choices that align with that definition.
10. Repeat.

You do not need a five-year plan, you need honesty. Listen to your pain. It is not weakness, it is information. Don't hide the problems. Don't numb them. Don't decorate them. Let them teach you. Surround yourself with people who want you to thrive, not just survive. Disappoint the ones who require your depletion.

Redefine success until it feels like peace. Make changes until your life reflects that peace.

When I was first asked to write about redefining success, I assumed I would write about career, income, achievement. That assumption alone revealed how deeply conditioned I was. Today, success is not something I achieve, it is something I connect with deep inside my heart and soul. It is alignment, integrity, presence, choice. True strength is not enduring endlessly. It is feeling, choosing differently, and being unapologetically me. And it all began the moment I listened and decided to live free.

Three

EMILY RAND

DEDICATION

This chapter is dedicated to my family: my husband, children, parents, sister, niece, nephew, and in-laws. You have taught me the true meaning and importance of a Joyful Home, and for that, I am forever grateful. And to my Joyful Homes clients, thank you for creating space in your homes and hearts for our decluttering and organizing journey. Your openness and trust have inspired me to share my own story. Success isn't about perfection, it's about choosing to start and committing to yourself. We are brave, and we can do hard things!

EMILY RAND

Emily Rand is the founder and owner of Joyful Homes. She is a trained professional organizer who is passionate about helping people experience the transformative power of an organized home. Since 2023, she has been dedicated to guiding busy families, professionals, and retirees through the process of decluttering, organizing, and creating space for joy in their homes and lives. Through her JOYFUL Method™, Emily blends her knowledge in physical and health education with her own experience as part of the "sandwich generation"—being a mom of young children while simultaneously supporting aging parents—to create organizing systems that support clients' physical, emotional, and mental well-being. Her approach goes beyond just tidying up: she empowers her clients to build lasting habits that keep their homes organized and bring peace of mind. From in-person to virtual sessions, Emily's goal is to help her clients let go of what no longer serves a positive purpose in their lives to free up the space, time, and energy for what truly matters.

When she's not organizing or colour coding a closet, Emily enjoys being active with family and friends, moving and grooving to music, exploring the outdoors, and drinking coffee with a sweet treat.

Connect with Emily on Instagram

@joyfulhomes.ca or visit **www.joyfulhomes.ca**

FINDING JOY IN LETTING GO

Ten years ago, I was drowning in stuff. It was 2016, and I had moved my life from Ontario to the beautiful city of Victoria, BC, on Vancouver Island. At that point, I was living with my now-husband Mike, our cat, Mowgli, and our dog, Harley. Prior to the move, I had been working at a provincial health agency in Toronto when we decided to wander west to pursue the dream of easy living among the ocean, mountains, and forest. With backgrounds in physical and health education and kinesiology, the pull toward this active, healthy lifestyle felt only natural.

Within a month of moving, I started working at a national non-profit organization called Sport for Life. My role involved a lot of travel, as I delivered workshops and training sessions to sport coaches, recreation leaders, educators, and health professionals in communities across the province and country. Being an explorer and an extrovert, I loved this job and the opportunity it provided to connect with people of all backgrounds.

But while I was on the road and pouring all my energy into my job, our home started to suffer.

Piles of stuff started to build. There were papers to deal with, knickknacks and decor items I had been haphazardly collecting throughout my twenties, and clothes from the past that no longer reflected who I was becoming—personally or professionally.

I started feeling the clutter creep into my mind, making it foggy and unshakable. When I woke up every morning, these piles were staring at me. When I returned from work, they were waiting for me. When I tried to relax or go out to enjoy the activities we had moved to the Island for, they reminded me that I had something on my to-do list first.

Despite all my cleaning efforts—vacuuming, dusting, wiping surfaces—the piles of stuff did not disappear. They only got moved around within the house.

Soon, the physical clutter became the mental clutter. I was drained.

It was on a particularly exhausting and defeating day that I knew something had to give. I had to get on top of the clutter before it completely consumed me. Coincidentally, it was also in this year of 2016 that the Japanese tidying guru Marie Kondo released her infamous book *Spark Joy: An Illustrated Master Class on the Art of Organizing and Tidying Up*. I can't exactly remember how or where I picked up this book, but the fact that it landed in my hands was a true "meant to be" moment.

That evening, I started reading it and quickly became captivated by her decluttering and organizing method, as her philosophy and practical tips resonated with how I wanted to approach and tidy my home.

It was fairly straightforward:

- Tidy by category so you know your inventory.
- Keep the items that bring you joy.
- Designate an intuitive home for each item you keep.
- Say farewell and let go of the rest with gratitude.
- And by the end of your "Tidying Festival," you will be surrounded by everything that you love, need, and use.

As soon as I finished reading her book, I felt motivated, committed, and ready to dive into my own "Tidying Festival."

Starting with my clothes, as was suggested in this method, I collected every item from every closet and drawer. Once my search was complete, what I faced was a *huge* pile on my bed and floor that felt embarrassing and shameful to look at. There were items

I hadn't worn in years. Items I had completely forgotten about. Items that straight up made me feel guilty for the memories they held, the wasted money I had spent, or the ways in which my body had changed over time.

I took a moment to sit with these feelings.

And then, I started picking out my favourites.

It may sound strange to start with the favourites, as we often go right to what's "wrong" and needs to be discarded when decluttering. But I trusted this method and recommendation to start by finding what's "right." Within a minute, I had my top three picks. When I held them, my body and face exuded joy. I loved the way these pieces felt and looked. They became my gold standard for clothes to which I then compared all other items. It was important to become attuned to this feeling of joy, as it guided my decision-making. Slowly but surely, I picked up one item at a time and made my way through the mound of clothes.

As I went through the decision-making process, I created five piles:

- Keep
- Donate
- Garbage / textile recycling
- Sell / consign
- Return / give to friends or family (making sure that this was a very small pile as to not inundate others with *more stuff)*

When I was done "joy checking" all my clothes, I moved on to storing them properly. This meant storing items of the same category together (tops, bottoms, activewear, work wear, etc.), using a specific technique of "file folding" clothes in the drawers, hanging clothes in the closet on the same types of hangers for a consistent look, and arranging them by colour for an even more organized aesthetic.

I packed up all the discarded items and committed to having them out of the house and off to new homes within the week.

When I opened my closet and drawers the next day, I couldn't believe it. I loved everything! The way the clothes looked, the way they felt to me, and how well everything functioned. I don't know if I had ever felt this way about my wardrobe before.

In the coming weeks, I made my way through decluttering and organizing other major and minor categories of our home:

- Books
- Papers / files
- *Komono* (Japanese for "miscellaneous," which includes a number of subcategories like kitchen, bathroom supplies, holiday decor, sport / hobby equipment, etc.)
- Sentimental items (photos, life records, etc.)

These were the steps I repeated over and over:

- Bring all items of the same category together from throughout the house (not just from one room!).
- Joy check each item and decide what to keep with confidence, or let go with gratitude.
- Store like-with-like items.
- Put systems in place, like labelling, to maintain the organization over time.

After about two months, I completed my Tidying Festival. I had touched every single item in our home, decided whether it served a positive purpose and fulfilled a need in our life, and if so, found the right storage solution and home to put it in.

I felt amazing. A huge weight had been lifted off my shoulders. Suddenly everywhere I looked brought a smile to my face instead of a visceral stress response.

I knew:

1. **What we had.**
2. **Why we had it.**
3. **Where it belonged.**
4. **How to confidently let go of it once it outlived its purpose for us.**

Physically, I shed extra weight I had been carrying around from the stress the clutter was causing me. Mentally, I felt sharper, clearer, and energized. Emotionally, I had the capacity and bandwidth to give to others and myself again. I had created a Joyful Home, and I was extremely proud of myself.

And that's when I realized something profound. Clutter is simply postposed decisions about what to keep or let go of. And for items we keep, deciding on the best place to store them. And for items we let go of, deciding where to take them so that they *actually* get out of the house instead of lingering in a corner or the car trunk for another six months.

You see, clutter isn't a representation of our morals, values, or personalities. It is not inherently good or bad. It doesn't discriminate; it finds itself in homes of all sizes and demographics.

Clutter is a representation of the thousands of decisions we have to make on a daily basis: for ourselves, our family members, our jobs, our community. When we hit decision fatigue, as most of us do, it's usually our home that gets put on the back burner. These unmade decisions pile up in a way that is hard to deal with without a plan, method, or skills to do so.

For the following year, *Spark Joy* became my personal bible. I referred anyone I could to this book and method. In the fall of 2016, I flew home to Peterborough, Ontario, to help my parents through a three-day intensive decluttering and organization of their home, including their closets and basement. At one point, I stood in the middle of their packed basement, and for the first time, I fully appreciated that my sister and I had been using their home as a storage unit for our items—schoolwork, university furniture, sports equipment—for years. The task of decluttering was just as much our responsibility as it was theirs.

Category by category, item by item, I guided them through the decision-making, proper storage principles, and simple systems to put in place to stay organized. Without knowing it, my parents became my first unofficial Joyful Homes client.

Life continued on, and fast-forward to 2020. Not only was it the year the COVID pandemic started, it was also the year that we welcomed our first daughter, Willow, to the world. Her name was fitting for how adaptable and flexible we had to be in that tumultuous year. Birth plans changed, in-home postpartum supports were gone, and any sense of mother/baby community was overtaken by the fact that we were supposed to be living in isolated bubbles.

Then, in the spring of 2021, five years after moving out West, Mike and I decided it was time to move back to Ontario where our families were. As we packed everything up, I thanked our home for all the memories it had given us. Being grateful for each item was something I had cultivated through my Tidying Festival. I was also ready to declutter and let go of more at this point, knowing that we were entering a new chapter of parenthood and life.

After a U-Haul drive across Canada, we unpacked and settled into our new home in Collingwood, Ontario. I finished a year of maternity leave and then returned to my job at Sport for Life, but this time, I worked remotely and had a lot less travel. I toyed with the idea of finding a new job but knew we wanted to expand our family and figured it wasn't the best time to start something new.

In the fall of 2022, we welcomed our second daughter, Juniper, into the world. As the months went on in this maternity leave, an unsettling feeling started to creep in again. A feeling of overwhelm. Of too much stuff with not enough time or mental capacity to deal with it all.

I soon realized that the feeling of drowning in stuff that I had in 2016 was back. But this time, our home had changed. There were categories I didn't know how to declutter or properly store: toys, baby gear, kids' clothes of different sizes and seasons. And these were in addition to all the adult and pet items we were still managing.

I recall there were days on this maternity leave when I would drop my toddler off at daycare in the morning and dread going back to our house with our baby, knowing all the piles there waiting for me . . . demanding my attention, my decisions, and my energy that I definitely did *not* have during this sleep-deprived and hormonal time of life.

This continued on for a while until one night—similar to that time back in Victoria—I made the conscious decision that something had to change in our home before it completely consumed me.

I revisited my learnings from *Spark Joy* and dove into round two of my Tidying Festival; this time it was the Mom Edition. Again, I started with my clothes. I got real with where my "mom style" and body were at this stage in life and only kept the clothes that supported me in a healthy way. I joy-checked all our books, then decluttered all of our papers. In every free minute I had over the next month, I sorted, decluttered, and organized every category and area of our home.

Near the end, I could feel that familiar sense of joy and relief. I was beyond excited to feel like our home was under control again.

And that's when it hit me: **This is what success feels like.**

Not necessarily success that is tied to my work, or parenting, or relationships . . . but a *feeling of joy in my home.*

And then it hit me harder: This is what I wanted to spend my time and energy doing for work. I wanted to help guide others through their decisions in a way that is non-judgmental, empathetic, and rooted in a sound philosophy and beautiful approach that focuses on what's right versus what's wrong.

And so, during my maternity leave, I got trained in Marie Kondo's KonMari Method® of organizing. At the end of my leave, I returned to my job and Sport for Life part time, while also starting up Joyful Homes. I began helping young families, busy professionals, and retirees who were also struggling with the decision overload, the overwhelm, the stress of clutter.

In June of 2024, I decided to leave my non-profit job after eight years to go full time in Joyful Homes. This was not an easy decision to make, but if I had learned anything through decluttering, it was to trust my decision-making; to let go of what no longer served a positive purpose in my life to make space for something new.

I started to combine my training in the KonMari Method® with my personal experience and an ability to customize the decluttering and organizing approach for each client's unique home and lifestyle. The result has been the creation of my JOYFUL Method™, which includes:

Joyful Vision – helping you envision how you want your home or space to feel once it's organized

Open to Change – encouraging you to be open to change and to think differently about your space

Your Decisions – allowing you to be in full control of the decisions you make and providing expert guidance in this process

Functional Storage – finding storage solutions that function well and look great for your home and lifestyle

Upkeep with Systems – applying systems and teaching skills that help you maintain an organized home in the long term

Live Joyfully – in the end, you will be surrounded by the items that you love, need, and use; you'll know where everything belongs; and you'll have a home that is full of JOY!

The ultimate goal of Joyful Homes is to help others *find joy in keeping what they love—and feel the freedom of letting go of the rest*. I have redefined my own success in life and am on a mission to help others experience a similar sense of joy and freedom in their homes, and their lives.

Success Redefined is about a transformation from *overwhelm* to *joy.*
A physical shift from *a lot* to *just right.*
A mindset change from *scarcity* to *abundance.*
An emotional transfer from *ugh* to *ahhh.*

It's hard to articulate the impact that decluttering and organizing has on us. Through my own journey and working with clients, I have seen how it can change our health habits and lifestyle, give us confidence and trust in our decision-making, allow us to let go of relationships that no longer serve us, and welcome even better ones. Together, my clients and I have uncovered relationships with our belongings, bodies, finances, jobs, loved ones, and more. Tidying is an opportunity to understand why we hold on to items, and how to let go with gratitude.

Despite becoming a professional organizer with an acute attention to detail and appreciation for order, I have learned that **success is not about perfection. It's about being committed to yourself and intentional about how you want to spend your time and energy.** It's about deciding what you want to create space for, and what you can loosen the grip on. It's about surrounding yourself with the people and items you love, in environments that bring you joy. It's about freeing up the space, time, and energy for what and who you truly enjoy.

I recently came across a beautiful quote that epitomizes the Joyful Homes approach and my belief about success: **Happiness is found in three things: letting go of what was, enjoying what is, and having faith in what will be.**

So, does success always mean *having more*? Perhaps not. When it comes to our homes, and lives, success may actually look like having the right amount that feels good for us, functions well, and brings us a deep sense of joy.

Four

AMY SUSSEX

DEDICATION

This chapter is dedicated to my parents. Thanks for being a leading example that you can build something from nothing. To my husband, Rich, thanks for loving me, seeing me, trusting me, and being on this journey with me. To my two girls, Madelyn and Hannah, know that you can be, do, and have anything you desire. You are allowed to change your mind and can live your version of success. Know that I will always love you and be proud of you.

This chapter is also dedicated to the younger versions of me. The twenty-two-year-old who got a tattoo to remind herself to always believe in herself and was worthy of what her heart desired. The thirty-three-year-old who knew she couldn't stare at those four walls for twenty-two more years and was meant for more. To the thirty-six-year-old who walked away from corporate inspired but scared, knowing it all would make sense one day. To the thirty-nine-year-old dropping off her four-year-old at school and four-month-old baby at daycare, knowing it would mean something one day.

Remember that this is a journey, and the joy has always been in the journey, the version you are stepping into, and not always the goal you are striving for.

AMY SUSSEX

Amy Sussex is the founder of The Business Management Co., a small agency that supports female founders through strategy, systems, operations, and team management. She is also the host of the *Beyond Your Business* podcast, a space to share what it actually takes to lead in business and in life.

When she isn't behind the mic, networking, or working with clients, you can find her cheering on her kids at their latest sporting event, hanging by the beach, going for walks at the park, or training for her first HYROX competition.

Connect with Amy on Instagram **@amy.sussex**
on email at **amy@thebusinessmanagementco.com**
or visit **www.thebusinessmanagementco.com**

STOP CHASING AND START CHOOSING

Success used to look very different to me.

It looked like promotions, titles, being the one people could count on. It looked like doing the "right thing," following the expected path, and being praised for my strong work ethic and busy schedule. I used to wear my busyness like a badge of honour.

Then, one day at a chiropractic appointment, I mentioned that I wasn't feeling happy or fulfilled. And she asked me something that made me pause.

"When you think of your dream day, what are you doing?"

I remember describing my life exactly as it was in that moment: working as a supervisor in a corporate setting, wearing professional clothes, sitting at a desk in my office.

She looked at me and said, "Okay, well, if you're living out your vision now, then something else needs to shift if you aren't happy."

I wasn't sure what to say. I left there thinking I'd described my current reality, but I had never considered whether it's what I actually wanted. What vision did I have for myself? The truth was, I wasn't really happy with my career and the direction I was going, but I also didn't know any different. I didn't realize I was living someone else's version of success. I was doing what I thought I should. I kept climbing the corporate ladder because that's what society tells us we should do: "Get a good job with a pension and benefits. Then you'll be living the dream."

I've always been a leader, even when I didn't feel like one. I'm the oldest of three kids and the oldest grandchild on my mom's side of the family. From a young age, I was told that others were watching me. That I needed to be a good example. I think most older siblings carry this unspoken responsibility to be steady, dependable, and strong.

That pattern followed me everywhere. In most jobs I've held, I was the organizer, the problem-solver, the one people came to. I loved growth, development, and learning, and I was always searching for the "next thing," trying to figure out what I wanted to do with my life. What I learned very early on was this: Your work ethic matters.

My parents modelled that beautifully. My mom owned a flower farm business and worked tirelessly while still being present for us. My dad worked more than forty hours a week in his factory job and even more helping with the business. Hard work wasn't just encouraged, it was the norm.

But alongside that work ethic, something else developed. I became a people pleaser. I learned how to shrink myself to fit into situations. I didn't want to disappoint anyone. I didn't want to rock the boat. I often put my own needs last, rarely stopping to ask myself what I actually wanted.

Instead, I looked outward for validation. I was envious of people who seemed to know exactly what they were meant to do. I kept searching for the perfect fit, hoping someone else would tell me who I was and what I was good at.

On paper, I looked successful. Inside, I felt disconnected. This is the part of "success" no one really prepares you for: the moment when you realize you've done everything "right" yet it still doesn't feel right.

I had job security and people telling me I was doing great. But I felt restless. Heavy. What confused me was the guilt. I remember thinking: *Why isn't this enough? Why can't I just be grateful? Why do I feel like something is missing when nothing is technically wrong?*

This is where I believe many people abandon themselves. They tell themselves they're ungrateful or unrealistic, and they silence their inner voice instead of listening to it.

But that voice whispering *there's more* isn't asking you to burn your life down, it's asking you to pay attention. How do you explain something when all you have is an inner knowing, a feeling in your body you can't ignore, a quiet voice saying: *Keep going*.

My success started to crack. Between 2015 and the years that followed, things began to shift, slowly at first, then all at once. I had worked my way into a full-time supervisor role in my corporate job. The next logical step was manager. I had already been temporarily promoted into manager roles to cover leaves. From the outside, everything looked aligned. But inside, something felt off, which led me to having that conversation with my chiropractor.

I had become obsessed with perfection. I was always trying to please everyone: my staff, my manager, upper management, the union, my fellow supervisors. I was carrying so much responsibility and emotion that I didn't even realize how heavy it had become.

I wasn't fulfilled. And worse, I felt like I was meant for more but didn't know what "more" was. I remember sitting in a board meeting staring out the window and having this wave rush over me as I thought, *Who am I? How did I get here? Is this really what I want to do for the rest of my life?*

I had already been working for this company for years and ignoring the whispers to explore something else. I knew this wasn't it but didn't know what was. *How can I leave something like this? What will people think? What will people say?*

That's when the panic attacks started. At the time, I didn't know that's what they were. I thought I was having a stroke. My body would shut down, my chest would tighten, and then it would feel like I was going to pass out or my face was going to fall off.

Once, in a staff meeting, I was partway through a presentation when my hands went numb and I couldn't breathe. I couldn't collect my thoughts, and I couldn't speak. I remember shaking and feeling really wobbly, like I was having an out-of-body experience. I abruptly left the meeting and walked outside and around the building. Then I went back into the room. As much as it terrified me, as nervous as I was of judgment and embarrassment, I knew I had to go back in there. I finally realized in that moment that I was out of alignment in my life, and it had finally caught up with me after ignoring it for years.

I made a doctor's appointment because I was convinced something was seriously wrong. He told me I was experiencing generalized anxiety and panic attacks. I remember thinking, *Nope. That's not me. Something else is seriously wrong.*

And in a way, I was right. Something *was* seriously wrong—my mental and emotional state—and it had started showing up physically. I tried medication, hoping it would help. Instead, I felt worse. Depressed, numb, and ashamed. I remember one Sunday in February, I was lying on the couch feeling depressed and anxious. I thought, *There is no way we are supposed to live like this.*

I dreaded going into work. I usually had the "Sunday Scaries" the night before going to work the next day. Then they started creeping into my Sunday mornings, then the moment I woke up. I had so much shame and guilt around these feelings because I kept telling myself I should be so grateful to have the career I had. I felt like I had lost my voice.

What I didn't realize then was that I wasn't losing my voice—I was finding it. It had just been buried for a very long time.

I knew what I didn't want and how I wanted to live my life. I also knew only I had the power to change things. No one was coming to save me; it was on me to make a choice and to choose something different. So, I did. I started making small changes to help my mood.

I changed who I surrounded myself with.

I became more intentional about what I watched on TV and listened to on the radio.

I moved my body more.

I explored holistic therapies.

I stopped the medication.

I started meditating.

I began journalling, reflecting, practising gratitude, and asking myself a question I had avoided for years: *What do I actually want*?

One of the biggest moments came when I declined a manager role. I sat down with my director and manager and told them that this wasn't the career progression I wanted at that time. That conversation felt terrifying.

I could feel their disappointment. And for someone who spent her life trying not to disappoint anyone, this was a massive step. But deep down, I knew I needed to figure out who I was and not who I was expected to be.

Throughout this journey, it was also terrifying sharing with my husband that I wanted to leave my corporate job and do something else. He didn't quite understand it, but he was supportive and wanted to see me happy. I felt like I now had to prove to him, to myself, to our family and friends that I could create something and be successful.

When I became pregnant with my first daughter and knew I would be going on maternity leave, I began brainstorming a new option. I knew I couldn't go back full time, and with a child on the way, I had even more reason to choose what made me happy and a better parent. So, I took courses during her naps and read business books after her bedtime. I learned about the impact of social media on business today and told my mom how her beautiful flower farm would have been so popular on Instagram.

As I reflect now, I can see that I was moving through change using the same four-step process even before I realized what it was I was actually doing.

It wasn't strategic—it was intuitive, emotional, and messy. This led me to starting my own wellness business in 2018, then shifting into business consulting in 2023. This process allowed me to fully step into what I feel I was always meant to do.

I call it my **4-Step Redefinition Process**:

1. **Excite** – Spark the vision
2. **Eliminate** – Remove what's not aligned
3. **Explore** – Test and experiment
4. **Execute or Elevate** – Implement with intention

1. EXCITE – WHEN SOMETHING PULLS YOU FORWARD

Excitement doesn't always feel light and joyful. Sometimes it feels uneasy. Overwhelming. Even chaotic.

Sometimes it feels disruptive.

Sometimes it creates more questions than answers.

Sometimes it shows up as dissatisfaction before desire.

For me, excitement often came disguised as discomfort, a feeling that I had outgrown something before I knew what was next.

This step isn't about clarity. It's about honesty.

Honesty about what energizes you.

Honesty about what drains you.

Honesty about what no longer fits, even if it once did.

Every major transition in my life started here: leaving corporate, entering the wellness world, then leaving wellness to move into consulting. Career changes. Relationship changes. Identity shifts.

The question isn't "What's the plan?" it's "What's pulling me?"

Excitement and curiosity are often the first signals that something is possible even if you don't know how it's going to work yet.

2. ELIMINATE – THE PART NO ONE TALKS ABOUT

This is where things get real.

The important thing to know is this:

Step two often feels the hardest.

It's uncomfortable. Heavy. Stretching. But that doesn't mean you're doing it wrong.

Eliminating isn't just about removing tasks, it's about releasing thoughts, patterns, people, habits, and expectations that no longer fit.

Who are you without the title?

Without the role everyone praises you for?

Without being needed?

This step brought grief for me: Grief for versions of myself I had worked hard to become. Grief for past identities and who I was becoming. Grief for releasing the people-pleasing identity.

I've eliminated:

- Clients that feel heavy
- Conversations that drain me
- Foods that don't support my body
- Circles that are no longer aligned
- Beliefs that tell me I'm not enough

This step feels uncomfortable because you're shedding layers of who you used to be, something that can feel like loss before it feels like freedom.

3. EXPLORE – STRETCH BEFORE YOU DECIDE

Exploration is where you give yourself permission to try.

You put yourself in rooms that stretch you.

You take courses.

You have conversations.

You experiment without needing certainty.

This is when I joined network marketing in 2016. Took courses in 2017 and 2018. Registered my business in 2018. Tested ideas. Failed. Adjusted.

Exploration doesn't require commitment, it requires curiosity and the courage to try.

4. EXECUTE OR ELEVATE – LIVING THE DECISION

This is where you check in.

What's working?

What needs refining?

What systems support you now?

Execution isn't about hustle. It's about intention. Elevation is about optimization. And sometimes, success is simply choosing again. For most of my life, I knew how to lead others, but I didn't know how to lead myself. The year that changed this was 2025. I was leaning into an old identity, a proving mentality.

I thought I'd feel successful when I reached a certain income. That I was a legit business and business owner. I went to bed December 31, 2025, and I realized not only had I earned that amount, I'd surpassed it! But in that moment when I reached my goal, I didn't feel different. I felt neutral about it; no more or less. That's when I realized it isn't about money. It's about who I am, how I show up, the journey I am on, and the impact I can make.

Looking back, what has made me successful is the time I've spent for me, the confidence I've gained, the lives and businesses I've helped to support, my family, going to the gym, the person I'm being and becoming, the relationships I've formed, and the community I surround myself with daily.

Leading myself required unlearning: Unlearning my belief that my worth was tied to productivity. Unlearning my habit of over-explaining my choices and the need to be accessible at all times.

I began asking different questions:

- What do I want my days to feel like?
- Where am I abandoning myself to keep peace?
- What version of me am I modelling for my children?

That last one really hit me hard! This is when success stopped being something I chased and started being something I practised.

I set boundaries with clients.

I set boundaries with family.

I scheduled gym time twice a week, a non-negotiable. I had a health scare that reminded me how often I put myself last and was pausing my life.

As a mom, wife, and business owner, I wore so many titles that I lost sight of who *Amy* was. I wasn't sure I ever truly gave her the space to exist. I realized I had been chasing titles, status, money, and approval. It was like high school worries all over again: fear of judgment, of disappointment, of not being enough.

I asked myself: *What if success isn't about proving anything? What if it's about choosing myself, over and over again?*

That's when I realized success was never the destination; rather, it's the relationship I had with myself along the way. Success, for me, started becoming about trusting myself enough to take the next step even when I didn't know exactly where it was going to take me. Success doesn't magically happen overnight. It's a series of small decisions that compound over time.

I used to believe success meant being busy and needed; I was constantly proving myself. Now, success means being present, honest, and aligned. I want to be the proof and a legacy for my daughters that you can do what you love, and you are allowed to change your mind, grow and evolve, and live life now. **Success isn't something to chase, it's a choice to make.** It means leading my life with the same intention I once used to lead everyone else. It's trusting your inner knowing to have the hard conversations before everything collapses at once.

Success is leading your own life even when it's scary and doesn't make sense or seem logical to the outside world. And once you decide, all it takes is one small step. Then another. And another.

For a long time, I thought redefining success meant making a bold move, quitting, changing everything, and starting over. But what I've learned is that most redefinitions don't happen in one dramatic moment. They happen slowly and quietly, in the conversations you finally have and in the boundaries you stop apologizing for. They happen when you start honouring what your body, mind, and intuition have been telling you all along.

Redefining success isn't about being fearless, it's about being honest about the version of yourself you're ready to become. If you're feeling the sense that something is off even though everything looks fine, trust yourself. I want you to know that you are not behind and you're not broken. Believe that you are standing at the edge of a new definition and make your choice.

Five

ASHLEE LIVINGSTONE

DEDICATION

This book is dedicated to my biggest loves: my wife, Kate, and my biggest win, my son, Miller. You are my everything, and your love reminds me every day that really, I already have it all! The life we are building and the fun we have is something I know I will be proud to see when it all flashes before my eyes. To Andrew, thank you for being in this co-parenting journey with me. We decided to stay connected to raise our boy together, and I'm proud we are doing that. Talk about staying regulated!

To my clients, I love guiding and supporting you and have learned so much from you all and feel so grateful that you have trusted me with your goals, vision, and heart. You have allowed me in, and I know this is sacred. To my mentors, Heather, Amanda, and Catherine, I want to be you when I grow up! Thank you for challenging me, believing in me, and calling me on my BS. I borrow your belief often and for that I am grateful. To my fellow co-authors, this has been so fun to do with you and there isn't a group of amazing women with whom I'd rather be in a book.

ASHLEE LIVINGSTONE

Ashlee Livingstone is the founder of Ashlee Livingstone Coaching, a personal growth and breathwork coach supporting high performers who are reaching for their next level in life and business. She teaches her clients how to stay regulated to enhance their clarity and focus, supports them as they navigate resistance, and ensures they are empowered as they take action toward their next level.

Ashlee is the creator of The Mental Fitness Club—a space to breathe, actively destress, and regulate—a program supporting high performers and teams (from entrepreneurs, women in business, athletes, and first responders), where she guides them through the restorative process of becoming regulated to improve their performance and quality of life.

With a background in event and people management, as well as having certifications in trauma-informed breathwork facilitation and life inventory assessment coaching, Ashlee combines somatics with strategy in her work. She understands that both are required to fully align and take action toward goals (whether that's a good night's sleep, staying present with your family, or stepping on the stage to share your voice). Ashlee is known for creating space for deep insight, clarity, and safety.

When she's not facilitating breathwork or creating alignment plans for clients, you'll likely find Ashlee with her family by the water in Ontario, taking fun road trips to discover another craft brewery, or watching (and playing) baseball.

Connect with Ashlee on Instagram **@ashlee.livingstone**
or visit **www.ashleelivingstone.com**

RELEASING THE INNER CRITIC

The negative voice in my head was so loud that night. I lay in the bathtub, refilling my glass of wine, overcome with grief and regret after yet another failed fertility cycle. A miscarriage this time.

I was consumed by my own shame, anger, and disappointment, but most of all, the story that I was just not good enough to have a baby. My inner critic was doing a number on me: telling me this was all my fault, I deserved this pain, and I wasn't the type of person who got what she wanted. I was at war with that voice, which is how I felt most of my life.

I feared my inner critic. She was loud, mean, defensive, and quick to anger. I lived being stuck with her, trying anything and avoiding everything in order to not be judged by her. But that rarely worked, as I constantly felt wrong, not good enough, and disappointed with myself.

She kept me on the sidelines of my life to avoid the failure I feared. She kept me distant and disconnected from other people, fearing their rejection while also projecting my anger onto them. She kept me lonely and doubting myself, fearing any mistakes and embarrassment. I constantly complained about others to deflect her criticism. She kept me in conflict to distract me from the sadness I felt. She kept me on the fringes of my life, never fully "all in" to save me from the vulnerability of failure and her judgment.

Because of her, I defined success as survival, a checklist, a predictable path, absent of bumps, detours, or breakdowns. She defined success as "normal" and sticking to the predictable plan everyone else followed. The known enemy vs. the unknown stranger.

There was nothing in this definition about embracing your feelings and life's moments with deep presence, going on adventures without a plan, changing your mind, enoughness, mistakes that become learning, powerful pivots, navigating disappointments, winding roads, the path less travelled, juicy self-awareness and growth, boundaries that set you free, transformational silence, and healing that you didn't even know you needed.

There was nothing about spaciousness, letting go, not caring what everyone thinks, hugs that last forever, and "yeses" that change your life. There was nothing about taking risks, pushing yourself, or slowing down and trusting yourself more than anyone else.

This memory of hiding in the bath sums up perfectly how I dealt with things—*alone*. I didn't dare share with anyone because I was too afraid to have my fear of not being good enough validated. I wish I could say that on that night I'd had enough of my inner critic and decided then and there to silence her, but that's not how it went for me. The truth is, I continued to live with her for several years, knocked down, stalled, and often stuck in believing her stagnant definition of success.

You see, for me, I didn't know I needed to stop listening to the negativity because I truly thought it was just who I was. So, while I did eventually become pregnant and became a mother to my son, my inner critic didn't see this "win" but rather quickly shifted to identify more areas where I was not "doing it right."

When people talk about the change of becoming a mother, they most often talk about your body changing, your sleep being affected, your focus and priorities shifting. What they don't talk about enough is how it will bring up so much of your own wounds. So many damaging stories that often feel like you are failing as you are trying to survive. It's a messy cocktail of stress.

I didn't realize how much becoming a mother would (and still does) test me, mirror back my insecurities, and let the narrative of that negative inner voice flow. In the early days of motherhood, when I was home all day with a newborn, I had the desire to do things "differently" and "right." But I fell into the exact same pattern as always. I felt exhausted, frustrated, and, once again, "not good enough." Motherhood became a spotlight for me on what wasn't working in my life. Raising a human will absolutely highlight for you what is unhealed, the stories that shape your perspectives, the fears you have, and what you believe about yourself.

If motherhood wasn't enough fuel for my inner critic, adding "business owner" into the mix created a field day of self-judgment, fear, stress, and scarcity. I often wanted to hide or just blow it all up. Listening to the nagging whispers of "Why can't you figure this out?" and "Nothing comes easy for you" persisted and got louder.

I launched my first business, a fundraising and event management company, while I was on maternity leave. It was a natural step from my corporate role, where I was the lead planner for fundraising events for a local hospital foundation. I created my company with a partner who was also on maternity leave. A win-win.

My "why" was rooted in wanting to spend more time with my son. It had taken me so long to bring him into my life that I couldn't tolerate going to a job where I cried in the parking lot or had to pep talk myself out of the car every day and not get to have that time with him. So, to say I was excited about the prospect of quitting my corporate gig would be an understatement. But I was not equipped for the constant negative nattering that added to my stress about money, feeling rejected by the "nos," feeling the pressure to do more for the clients I did have, and judging myself for not being a fully present mom. I felt like I was sucking at both running a business and being a mom. The ever-present guilt only fuelled my inner critic. It really seemed that I could not win.

I can see now how these beliefs held me back, only to prove my inner critic right. With little to no boundaries, working more than ever but earning less, and zero flexibility, I second-guessed myself and trusted myself less and less.

Over the course of my journey of where motherhood meets entrepreneurship, I started to feel so boxed into this life I had created. It was like I was stuck on autopilot—just doing, repeating, doing and repeating. It wasn't that it was "bad," it just wasn't fully living.

I remember landing a client who ran retreats for female entrepreneurs. It was the first time I was around women who were investing in themselves, supporting one another, sharing their struggles, and setting bold goals. I think I was most intrigued by the idea that they were rooting for one another. I hadn't been a part of something like this before, and even still, I was looking in from the outside. I was organizing it. I wasn't experiencing it. This is when something began to slowly shift for me. I remember feeling curiosity and hearing another voice, a faint whisper that said, "There's another way."

The idea of success began to shift for me. I know I started to consider that there was another way. That I could have . . . more.

For me, *more* began to look like redefining work by considering ways to scale and expand, to join groups and learn. *More* also looked like opening myself to love, which led to meeting my wife, Kate.

In 2020, during the pandemic, when I was running my business solo after my business partner and I decided to go our separate ways, managing pivot after pivot and virtual event after virtual event while navigating virtual school with my son, in grade two, I decided to invest in my first business coach.

My inner critic *freaked out* when I paid for this. There was *a lot* of self-judgment and fear that came with this investment. I even tried to get out of the contract by again second-guessing myself, fearing I had made the "wrong" decision and telling myself I couldn't afford it.

I didn't, it wasn't, and I could!

My coach was big on the "give you what you need, not what you want" approach, and while I wanted business templates, strategies, things I could "do" to improve my business, she invited me to explore my *why*, the feeling I was after, and my core desires. What?! How was this going to help me grow my business? And then she invited me, and the others in the program, to experience breathwork.

I quickly resisted, my inner critic shouting things about "woo" and "not useful." I wanted a plan to fix whatever was wrong with me and my business, I didn't want to feel or release, and I definitely didn't want to slow down and breathe (insert eye roll). But I trusted my coach (more than I trusted myself), so I joined the group call.

When the facilitator started the breathwork journey, my body resisted at first, struggling to stick with the breath pattern and getting distracted by thoughts. I was still in my head, wondering if the others were watching and judging me. But I stuck with it and started to settle in with the rhythm of my breath and the gentle guidance of the facilitator. I focused on my breath, and I was moving into it when I started to hear some of my biggest fears, the ones I avoided at all costs:

You are all alone.

You are never going to figure it out.

You are not good enough to run your own business.

As my body felt that, I experienced tightness, tears, and anger, then the resistance came—I wanted to stop, run, hide. But then, just as quickly, something shifted. My (late) grandmother came to me so clearly. She placed her hands on my face and looked directly into my eyes. I felt this wave of safety all over my body. Then I heard this tiny whisper: "You are okay. You are not alone."

The comfort of that moment, the presence I felt, and the connection I had moved me to tears, allowing me to release so much pent-up fear and tension. And I felt peace. Maybe for the first time ever. Afterward, I thought: *How do I get more of that?!*

My first experience with breathwork got me curious. What or who was I hearing? How did breathing help me feel so safe? I felt so connected to my grandmother—the person I knew loved me unconditionally—it felt like I could *feel* her hands on me. That was something I wanted again. So, I continued to practice. I built thirty minutes into my morning routine to breathe and journal. It was through this consistent practice that I discovered exactly what I had heard initially. **It was my inner voice**.

At first, she was so quiet. It was hard to hear over the noise of my inner critic, but with practice, I got better at creating space to listen. **I began to notice, over time, that when I followed my breath, my body began to welcome the calm. The noise would quiet down, and in this space, I could hear what I now know as my inner voice.**

I learned that my inner voice is calm, compassionate, and encouraging. She believes in me, guides me toward choice, alignment, and fulfillment (something I didn't know mattered to me as much as it does now).

I had gotten so stuck with my inner critic that I didn't know I had an inner voice. I actually thought the critic *was* my inner voice. I believed I was just a negative person and that things didn't work out for me. I thought I was an angry girl who wouldn't find peace. I thought this unhappiness was what being an adult was because that was all I knew. I didn't realize I was just stuck in survival patterns and was very unregulated. It's uncomfortable to admit, but I really believed this. It wasn't just a bit of "a funk" or a tiny period of time. I'd felt this way for as long as I can remember. The critic collected more and more proof as I moved through my life, and the negative stories became my reality. Just writing these words and remembering how deeply I identified with my inner critic makes me feel sad about how much of my life I was stuck with this isolating voice that held me back from so much.

And this is how it works. The stories we are told, we take in. Then, we believe them, and if we don't release them or challenge them, they shape our actions and we become a representation of them. We start to live these stories as if they were true all along. We memorize them and play them on repeat, and our subconscious finds proof that makes it somewhat impossible to challenge.

We all have a filter that only sees what we believe. I remember identifying this story: Money doesn't come easily to me. And then sure enough, I'd find proof of it: from my student debt to my low-paying jobs, to the expensive fertility treatments to the clients who said no. Everything was all proof that money was hard for me to make, keep, or build.

I realize now I spent so much time listening to the wrong channel. I was defined by a version of success that didn't really serve me. The volume was so loud on the inner critic's station, I couldn't hear my inner voice. But once I started giving myself space to breathe, my body relaxed, it felt safe to be still, and my critic quieted so my inner voice felt safe to be heard.

And the biggest shift was that now I was listening. Slowly over time, the volume adjusted. I began to hear my inner voice so much more clearly, even in the chaos of everyday life.

As I learned to listen deeply to myself, one of the aha moments I had was that in planning events for others to shine and be seen, I was hiding myself. I'd write scripts for other people, plan award ceremonies for them to be celebrated, and create experiences for other people to enjoy, all while I was in the background. In fact, I used to pride myself in saying at events: "If no one knows I was here, then I did my job."

This message stopped serving me when I listened deeply to my inner voice and realized I actually wanted to be seen, heard, and connected.

So, I bravely leaned into this desire by launching my business: Ashlee Livingstone Coaching, where I use my formal breathwork training and certification, life alignment certification, and a whole lot of life experience to help others discover their inner voice and create lives they don't want to avoid anymore.

I know I'm on the right path now, as my whole self gets so lit up when I create space for someone to learn about themselves, to experience true calm, to finally hear themselves think and relearn how to trust themselves. I know how powerful this journey is that I guide women on because I've been on it myself. I now get to help others redefine success and love the shit out of their lives.

One of the most important things I've discovered is that whenever I slip into stress, overwhelm, or pressure, my inner voice quiets down and my inner critic once again runs the show. This essentially puts me back into old survival patterns and tells stories that I know on a logical level don't support me or those around me. The difference is, I don't stay there as long now because I know how to shift and get my truest self back in the driver's seat.

We cannot think clearly when we are overly stressed or in survival mode, so we do what we know. We fall back into coping strategies that protect us: we yell, get defensive, avoid, resist, deflect, or numb ourselves.

Breathwork is one of the fastest ways to shift this and help us get regulated. It allows us to feel calm, grounded, and clear.

And from this calm space, you will have greater clarity and be able to cut through the noise, fear, and confusion. With clarity, you will be able to access ideas, choices, and options that feel aligned for you—where you understand your priorities and what feels best for you.

With clarity and alignment, it becomes easier to let go of the resistance, limiting beliefs, and patterns holding you back.

I am a big advocate for letting go of what no longer serves you to create capacity for more of what does. This is a staple message inside many of my guided sessions! And once you understand what to let go of, you can move forward with confidence and self-trust.

This has been a journey and it's one I'm still on. I'm constantly challenged by my inner critic, and I have healing and growth still to do, but with my inner voice on my side, I feel so much more supported. I am constantly reminding my clients and myself that growth isn't a one-and-done strategy or an instant gratification moment. It's a continual practice!

My inner critic is not gone, but it is definitely quieter these days. And I can decipher between the two. I can recognize when fear, the feeling of less than, and disappointment are making decisions and I need to STOP. STOP has become another tool for me that I use quickly in all sorts of moments. There are lots of versions of STOP, but being the creative entrepreneur that I am, I made my own version. This is meant to help you STOP before you react automatically, before you say yes, before you slip into overwhelm, before you yell, before you hide.

For my clients and me, STOP is a reminder to:

S: Slow down
T: Take a breath
O: Consider my **Options**
P: Proceed with <u>aligned</u> action

When I reflect on some of my life's moments in my highlight reel—having my son, starting two businesses, saying yes to Kate, trying breathwork, going on transformational retreats, becoming a breathwork facilitator, and saying yes to being a part of this book—they all have one thing in common: they were all results of me acting on the encouragement, the nudge of knowing, of my inner voice. Even when I couldn't hear it clearly, it was working with me, nudging me along, guiding me toward what I truly desired, and showing me that I do, in fact, deserve all that I wanted.

Now that I'm aware and listening, I am committed to never turning the dial down on my inner voice. Over time, I've developed greater self-trust, and I know that when I act from this place, I am doing so from self-love, self-trust, and alignment.

If I can help even one of you slow down long enough to take a breath and ask yourself: "What are my options?" and "What do I want to do that feels right for me?" then that's a win.

Learning to listen to my inner voice has been one of the most successful wins for me so far.

It has become the difference between *impulsive* and *intentional.*
Between *reaction* and *responding.*
Between *quantity* and *quality.*
Between *disconnection* and *connection.*
Between *confusion* and *clarity.*
Between *trapped* and *free.*

This gift of self-trust and self-connection is something I didn't think I'd have. But now I am so grateful for it. It is vital to building a life full of highlight-reel moments, moments I will be proud to see when they flash before my eyes.

To my younger self, the one in the tub who didn't know her inner voice was there, the one so afraid to feel, who feared her own self: Thank you for still moving forward. I'm grateful that despite the fear, the noise, the critic, you felt the nudge. You had hope in the hardest moments, and you kept showing up. When I look at my son, I feel so grateful for you.

If you are being held back by your inner critic, maybe even doubting there is a life without your negative narrative, I want you to know that while powerful and loud, your inner critic is not you. And if you give yourself permission, like I did, you can connect with your inner voice and hear your most beautiful, authentic thoughts, beliefs, and truths. And you, too, can begin to find the clarity in your life you are seeking. You can build deep self-trust and discover your next best step for you while building your life's highlight reel.

Six

ANDREA KRONES

DEDICATION

This chapter is dedicated to my two kids, Milo and Wyatt, so that they may have the confidence to dream big as they define their own version of success. And redefine it on their own terms, as often as needed, as they journey through life.

For all the creatives dreaming up a plan that feels out of reach, let this be your invitation to dream big, trust your gut, and find the confidence needed to define your own success.

ANDREA KRONES

Andrea Krones is the founder of Inkling Design, where she has helped business owners with graphic design and website projects since 2004. Alongside her business partner, Kelley Gibson, who she teamed with in 2018, Inkling has grown into a design and web agency helping heart-centred humans with their branding, websites, and marketing materials. They specialize in creating custom branding and WordPress websites for service-based businesses and non-profits on a mission to do good in their communities and beyond. They love empowering others to take control of their branding and website with confidence so they can stay in their zone of genius when scaling their business. Websites do not need to be overwhelming, and they can be beautiful and strategic at the same time.

In a world where people often choose the faster, cheaper, and less human approach to their marketing, Andrea listens to the person behind the brand before bringing their vision to life in a way that creates impact and connects with their audience.

When Andrea is not curating the perfect customer journey through a website or obsessing over the subtle differences felt within the perfect colour palette, you will find her exploring her neighbourhood in Guelph, spending time with family, or escaping on an adventure into the Ontario wilderness. You will almost always find her snacking on a bar of fair trade, organic dark chocolate.

Connect with Andrea on Instagram
@its.andrea.krones or visit **andreakrones.com**
Connect with Inkling Design on Instagram
@inkling.design or visit **inklingdesign.ca**

FROM INKLING TO ITERATION

For most of my life, I was a shy people pleaser who longed for validation but feared too much attention. Encouraged to dream big, then told to play it safe. As a perfectionist, an introvert, and someone with a hidden spark of independence with the drive to prove everyone wrong, my story was woven from these conflicting threads. The kind that are hard to tear apart.

So, what changed? How did I get from the quiet, cautious girl sitting in class shrinking so that I wouldn't get called on to becoming a successful agency owner who owns her expertise and delivers exceptional results to her clients? I didn't take the straight or quick path to where I am today. Defining my version of success was a slow journey, and I learned many lessons along the way.

While I loved creating throughout my life, I kept hearing the same message: You won't get a job doing art. I saw examples around me of talented people who knew what they wanted and went for it. The smartest kids in the class. The most talented kids in the class. There was always a comparison going on in my head. I couldn't draw as well as the best artist in the class, so I must not be a very good artist. If I wasn't the best, then it didn't count. Not that I strived to be the best. That would have attracted attention, and I was determined to stay under the radar.

Being conscientious, it didn't feel wise to go against the expectations and study art. So, I went into science, and specifically nutrition, because it seemed safe. You could get a job being a dietician. I didn't realize I was on the wrong path, and I desperately tried to make the nutrition program work for me. But there was resistance. Between needing to memorize a lot of formulas in biochemistry (turns out that is not my strength) to needing to read a lot of textbooks that never fully captured my attention, I knew I was forcing something that wasn't sitting right. Near the end of my second year of university, I was sick with mono and studying for my biochemistry finals. I was sitting in the middle of the floor in my tiny basement apartment, notes spread around me, textbook open, trying desperately to memorize all the organic compounds that were the basis for the upcoming exam. It was at that moment that I realized I was not cut out for science. I couldn't imagine forcing myself through another two years to get my degree. It felt like a failure from what my path *should* have looked like. But I was so lost on that path. **I knew it was the right decision, I just didn't know what the right direction was.**

It was around that time that I was pouring over different career paths that were not science, when I stumbled across graphic design. Why had no one ever told me there was a field I could study that required creativity, attention to detail, and where being conscientious could be an asset? I had taken so many career counselling sessions in high school and this never came up. Was I too cautious to create designs that would be out in the world for all to see? There was only one way to find out. That summer, while recovering from mono and two years at university that did not serve me, I enrolled in part-time courses at the local community college, in graphic design. For the first time, something clicked. I loved what I was doing! Was I a natural at it? I didn't think so. But I had the drive to see where it could take me.

After spending two years at university, I felt behind and didn't want to start from scratch with a four-year program in graphic design. Instead, I enrolled in an accelerated program that was only nine months long where, it turned out, most people who graduated didn't have enough skills or experience to be employable. They didn't share that on the brochure. But even with my caution, I was always driven. It can be a dangerous combination: too cautious to try but too determined to fail. The spark that was lit was enough to make me determined to get a job at the bottom and work my way up. The dream was a nine-to-five job where I was appreciated for my talents and skills, and where I could shine, be well-compensated, and work alongside other creative minds. It turns out that this dream was as realistic as me becoming a scientist.

My first career job had me working on direct marketing layouts (a.k.a. the junk mail addressed to you that no one reads). It was a bit soul crushing knowing the number of trees being converted to paper to create these campaigns that my twenty-one-year-old environmentally conscious self knew were not serving people. Taking public transit deep into the suburbs to work in a windowless office with easy listening adult contemporary playing on the radio was not the dream.

So, after putting in my time for two years, I found a better job in downtown Toronto for a home entertainment company. I liked movies and I liked downtown, so this felt like such a leap in the right direction. And for a time, it felt like a good fit. But I wanted more. My cautious side was grateful for what I had, but my driven side wanted to make a bigger impact, wanted more creative control, and wanted a raise. None of these things were happening.

I had started a side business, Inkling Design. I wanted to take my little idea, my *inkling*, and grow it into something larger. Like ink on a page, I wanted to create something meaningful and lasting. I was shocked that I was doing well. I felt like I had to prove myself to the world. Could the quiet introvert attract and retain clients? Deliver the work? Compete in such a busy and loud industry? I always had the drive to prove myself and the stubborn streak that would not let me fail. But what did that look like?

I had a growing list of clients, all from word of mouth, and to my surprise, I loved the challenge of presenting my ideas to a client, listening carefully to their goals, and creating exactly what they were looking for. Being thoughtful and empathetic were assets in an industry where there are a lot of louder voices. Being cautious, I wasn't charging my worth, not realizing that what I had was something worthy of a higher price tag. But I built up my clients slowly and steadily. Undercharging and overdelivering, thinking that was the definition of success. I was feeling a pull to explore freelancing further, and with every new project completed, I was one step closer to believing that running a successful freelance business was within reach.

I was busy, and wasn't that what I wanted? My dad ran his own business as a solopreneur, and I saw how hard he worked. His workdays were long: twelve-hour days Monday through Friday, plus five hours on Saturdays. Without knowing others who were self-employed, I took this as the standard. Running a business was hard work. You did what you loved, but you were all in, at any cost.

My weekends and evenings were filled with every type of project I chose to say yes to: logo design, websites, digital ads, and marketing materials. If it was a creative request, I accepted the challenge and did whatever it took to make it happen. Learn a new skill on my own time? No problem. Troubleshoot a request that sounded possible, even when I wasn't sure what the solution could possibly be? Sign me up. I was the only freelancer that I knew, so there was no one with whom to compare notes. I just did what I had to do to get clients, retain clients, and deliver over and above the promised results. The biggest problem with this model was the types of clients I was attracting. **When your secret weapon is your ability to do anything and undercharge, you end up attracting clients who expect that.** I don't regret this part of my journey since it taught me many lessons that may have been harder to learn any other way. But now that those lessons are carved into my memory, I won't be making those same mistakes again. Now, I can spot a "red flag client" from a mile away, and I can politely decline their projects. Once you know what it feels like to work with clients who value your time and expertise, there is no reason to accept anything less.

Taking the leap away from my steady income (even though it was lower than I deserved) felt risky. Maybe if I hadn't felt so underappreciated, I would have stayed safe. Maybe the biggest leap was only possible because of the curse of being undervalued.

I was slowly shrinking at my day job. Putting up my hand, trying to find ways to provide even more value, and working as hard as I could. I was trying to prove myself to a business that didn't want to hear what I had to offer. They liked me small, creating what needed to be created, earning the mediocre salary that followed me with modest increases over five years in my role as a junior graphic designer. I was torn between two worlds. Accepting defeat and living the nine-to-five life, overperforming without recognition, with bits of my soul and drive slowly dying. Or I could leave the stability of a secure job and go out on my own. Journey into the unknown, but know that at least I tried my best and if I failed it was going to be on my terms, not because a boss wouldn't give me a raise.

I decided to make one last big attempt at the raise I deserved. My drive to prove myself to them and to myself led the charge. I poured myself into a plan to prove my worth and ask for the raise I longed for. When I look back at my journey, one of the bravest moments was right there in my boss's office. Leading up to that meeting, I had filled out my performance review form as usual. But in the "Additional Comments" section, I made my last pitch. I wrote the most convincing argument I could.

I knew it was time to make the big ask and that if the answer was anything other than *yes*, then it was all the information I needed to make my next move.

I walked into the creative director's office and sat down. We both knew what was coming. I could see in her eyes that it wasn't going to happen. Her hands were tied, and they couldn't offer me what I wanted. After our conversation, I was holding back my tears and holding back my anger, but at the same time I had the deep knowing that I had tried my best and vowed to find something where I was valued.

Even with my freelance business growing, I wasn't quite ready to take the full leap. The lack of confidence ran deep, so I started looking at part-time graphic design roles, which felt like a safer stepping stone. I was too busy for full-time employment, and there were options for someone with my skills far beyond my current office walls.

It didn't take long to find a part-time graphic design position at a natural health supplements company in downtown Toronto. I gave my notice and that's when the higher ups asked if there was anything they could do to make me stay. It was a full body *no*. I told them it was too late and I had made my decision, and that was that. I was on to bigger and brighter things, and it felt great knowing I would be working two or three days a week for my new employer while focusing on my ever-growing freelance business on the side. This was a new level of success.

Being driven and working at a growing company led to the obvious: they wanted me to go full time. So, six months into my perfect arrangement, I had to make a big decision. I could either go full time with them and reduce my growing business back to an evenings and weekends side hustle again. Or I could finally go all in on Inkling Design. I gave both options some consideration, but I knew deep down in my heart that there was only one option. I followed my heart and went all in on my little business.

I felt lighter, excited, and so driven to see what I could make of my little inkling. It seemed like every time I made a decision to bet on myself and take a leap, my drive and determination led me to success. I needed more clients? I found them. I had hours in my day to spare? I filled them. But somewhere along the way I realized I was working very hard, and while it felt like success, it didn't leave much time for anything else. And when I made time for other things like outings with friends or exploring other creative hobbies, it always came at the expense of things that should have been non-negotiables, like sleep.

I didn't know other business owners trying to carve out their own path, so I didn't know any different. I carried on the busy-equals-success path for years. It wasn't until I was pregnant with my first child thirteen years ago that I had to reevaluate what being a successful business owner looked like. Not because I had the foresight to plan ahead, but because I had no other choice. There was some planning of course. While I had no plans to take a proper mat leave, I did realize that my sixteen-hour days were unsustainable with a new baby. I had hired freelancers here and there to support my workload over the years, but none had lasted more than a short-term contract or two. This time I knew I needed someone better to fill the gaps, and I hired a web developer who later ended up being my business partner after my second pregnancy.

Ten years ago, after the birth of my second child, I discovered the power of community. Along with my business partner, I joined my first online community for entrepreneurs who also happened to be mothers. It opened up a whole world of connections with people who get it (the challenges of running a business and raising tiny humans), and it showed me what was possible with the women who were further along on their journey. As I realized the power of community for both keeping me motivated and inspired, and for making me feel less alone, I joined other online communities too.

It was in this space and the power of community that I was finally able to evolve more as a business owner. When others started to see me as an expert in graphic design, UX design, and website design, I started to believe it too.

Being an expert doesn't mean being the absolute best in your industry. Expertise comes from your own unique perspective and the years it took you to get there.

When others saw me as a business owner rather than a freelancer, I believed it too. I was building something bigger than myself, and it was time to name what I was growing: a design and web agency.

As I leaned more on the power of community, I started attending many events for women entrepreneurs over the past couple years. Even as an introvert who loves spending my days quietly plugging away at creative projects at home, I still got so much out of being in the company of other women achieving amazing things. **Seeing what was possible for others made me start seeing more of what was possible for me.** Allowing myself to dream bigger. Giving myself time to curate the dream of what was important to me, like time spent in nature, time spent with my kids and partner, and the freedom to follow creative nudges to wherever they could take me.

Being a perfectionist comes with its own baggage. Like not fully trusting your own view of success and thinking you need to keep chasing what is always just out of reach. But where does this drive for the unattainable come from, and how can it be redirected toward good? What does peace with your trajectory look like after it is unpacked and built back up again as something that more closely resembles what you truly wanted all along?

Trying to figure out what you want means looking inward instead of outward. Catching yourself dancing across that line and stepping back where your feet feel comfortable and you can stand taller. And giving yourself grace, because undoing the years of conditioning also takes years to unravel.

I thought I needed every answer to every question before I could see myself as successful. I didn't pause to appreciate the journey because I was taught to seek the destination. But when the destination is a concept far in the future that you didn't dream up for yourself, it can be harder to grasp. When you don't pause long enough to dream up what that destination actually is, you get trapped in an in-between where success is harder to define, and impossible to find.

Success is trusting your gut. And then following your gut with your full heart, knowing and trusting yourself over all the noise, chasing, and grasping we are taught to follow. Becoming a leader in your own way, and following your own lead.

Success is confidence in self. The journey may be a long one, but every step brings more clarity, more intention, more wisdom, and ultimately, more success. A new success that you feel down to your core. It's sunshine on my face and the calming sounds of a late summer breeze. This is the success I want. No chasing, no hustling, just a deep knowing and contentment. What I have built lights me up. It gives me purpose. It fills my cup and allows me to pour into others.

I'm excited to see what the next iteration of success looks like for me. It's a journey and I get to define the markers. Not society. Not outside voices. Not the successes I see and celebrate around me. Not even the doubts that still try to creep in and take hold. Now I let them pass and don't give them my energy. I save that for me. For my journey. For my success.

My journey from that first inkling to accept a website freelance client has slowly led me all the way to the countless entrepreneurs and visionaries I help with turning their own inklings into impact.

Every time I bet on myself, my drive took me to the next stop along my journey.

Every time I questioned what success looked like to me, I realized I was allowed to redefine it. That's the beauty about success. The definition can evolve with you. Working sixteen-hour days felt like success to an older version of me. Without that version, I doubt I would be where I am today. So, I am grateful for her determination.

And I am grateful that I have evolved to appreciate that there can be impact without the overwhelm. That today's success will lead to a new version again in the future, and I am allowed to enjoy the journey and every stop along the way. **I changed course and learned so many lessons.** I took the long, slow journey from a side hustle that started as a mere inkling to a growing freelance main gig, to adding a business partner, an agency, a team, a community and most importantly, my definition of success.

Seven

CATHERINE FARQUHARSON

DEDICATION

This chapter is dedicated to all the women who dare to create their own rules and define their own terms for success. May we boldly claim a world of limitless possibility as we shed the old, outdated rules that were never meant for us in the first place. With each aligned move we make in this path to freedom, we affirm that we are the trailblazers, the quiet leaders, and the impact-makers who create the world we want to live in. We go first, the rest follows. We got this.

CATHERINE FARQUHARSON

Catherine Farquharson is a mindset and personal transformation coach who helps women redefine themselves as they redefine their next chapter. She has helped guide hundreds of women to evolve into their upgraded identity as they align with the truth of their hearts and dare to make the vision of their "impact years" come true. She is very casual and also very trained. Catherine is a certified trainer of neuro-linguistic programming, a trainer of Timeline Therapy™ Techniques, a trainer of HeartMath™, a master practitioner of hypnotherapy, a certified NIE practitioner, and a certified breathwork facilitator. Additionally, she is an avid student herself in this world and spends her "spare time" learning from the best in the world of manifestation and energetics, essential oils, embodiment, breathwork, polarity, and other esoteric rabbit-holes.

Connect with Catherine on
Instagram **@catherine_farquharson**
or visit **www.mindsetcoaching.ca**

RULES FOR SUCCESS AND A CASE FOR BREAKING THEM

The Rule of Noon: I don't meet with anyone before 12 p.m. No team meetings. No prospect meetings. No coffee connects. No emails. No phone calls. Just me and my mind.

This was the first business rule I ever set that really felt like mine. That I was making for me and how I wanted to run the ship. It felt bold and radical. *How audacious to declare yourself out of bounds until noon! How do you run a successful business that way?*

I didn't know if I could. **But I knew deep inside that if I could live by the terms that worked for me, then I would be far more successful than any hustle, grind, or burnout would ever bring.** I knew this because I'd be proud of the most important thing: not what I achieved, but who I was being as I built the business.

This is what it looks like now: I reluctantly wake at 5:45 a.m., roll myself out of bed, then zombie-walk my way over to my home office with barely an eye open. Fifteen minutes later, with essential oils diffusing away, warm lemon water in my mug, and the lighting "just so," I happily start my morning study. I follow this with a mix of journalling, meditating, ideating, and breathwork. If I need one activity more than another, I'll let my attention stay there longer. Sometimes I have all the content for an upcoming workshop start pouring out of me, and I'll use all the time to catch my notes. Sometimes I just sit there with a big question that has been circling, and I'll wait until a new answer comes to me. Sometimes my journal is just full of sentences that start with "What if . . ."

From there, the morning might take me to a forest walk with my dog, coffee with my husband, exercise, breakfast, or something else I feel like doing. Sometimes it's an activity related to working *on* the business, sometimes it's not. I honour myself in this way so when I start working *in* the business at noon, I enter in as the best version of myself: *I have already had the best day. Now, let's get to work!*

Once I give my attention over to others, I have switched to Action Mode: responding to emails, whatever action item is needed, or the tasks assigned to that day.

The morning spaciousness isn't to "get somewhere" or do something because apparently, "I'm supposed to." It is about honouring myself, tending to my needs, and assuring there is thought, feeling, and action alignment. I coined the term for this morning practice: Devotional Discipline. I wanted the name of my activities to emphasize why I do this as a daily reminder.

I have come to know that this is required for my success now. I am seeing oh-so-clearly in hindsight. The truth is, it was years before I let myself run my business this way. Before you can be an "unconscious competent" (being so naturally good at something you have no awareness of it), you have to first be an "unconscious incompetent" (unaware and not good at it). Then, you become a "conscious incompetent" (aware now, but still not good at it), and eventually you practice your way along until you strengthen those muscles to the level of "conscious competent" (aware that you're good at it). Over time, the fact that you are competent seeps in so deeply that you finally lose awareness of it. It's the long and unfortunate process of change and growth, and you just can't skip it.

My relationship to my morning was the window where I could see how I was unconsciously running my business. Before the Rule of Noon, or any self-created rules at all, I was doing a morning routine as I had always done it. I have been a lifelong journaller, so it has always been part of my practice. And in my morning hour I had allotted, I could do some journalling and a short, guided meditation if I was alert enough at the start. I would give myself barely an hour a day and truthfully, I was still feeling like I never had enough time. But as 9 a.m. approached, I had to get ready for my day. I thought I didn't have a choice.

This is how indoctrinated I was: Do the thing you're "supposed to do" in the morning and start the workday at 9 a.m. sharp because that's the start of the workday. Everyone who is successful does that, it's been said. Bonus points for posting about it on social media so everyone can see how effective you are. Now you will be successful.

I really wasn't thinking for myself, not really. I wasn't taking my own preferences and strengths into account, such as when my "genius zone" time is or even asking myself what I really wanted. I was just following along with the rules, doing the thing that you're supposed to do without questioning it. It never occurred to me that I could give myself permission to change my start time. Not really, and not that dramatically. Even as a business owner who technically can make her own rules, I was still living by these all-encompassing restrictions that someone I can't name set at some point in history.

Now, I'll start by saying that you don't go into my field of mindset and personal transformation coaching if you aren't ready for the fast-track on personal development and evolution. This is not a career that anyone should go into because of some illusion that it appears lucrative or easy. This is a career that is the most illuminating, humbling, and, if lived authentically, the most confronting. I like to joke that it's a great career for anyone looking to complete their last lifetime on Earth and finally face all their demons once and for all.

I could have continued in this morning routine and no one would have noticed. Nothing was wrong. It was a perfect match to the identity I was living and the results I was getting. And it was perfectly acceptable behaviour because it followed the rules of productivity. But you know the saying "The way you do one thing is the way you do everything"? If I was bypassing my true preferences and needs in something as simple as the time I started my workday, where else was I doing it?

When I started to look, I could see it everywhere. I was living my life and running my business by everyone else's rules that came from business books, podcasts, business coaches, etc. After that, I couldn't unsee it. As it turns out, I had a whole invisible "Successful Business Rulebook" where my rigid start time was just one of the rules. I blindly followed these "rules" even when they contradicted one another:

- Map out your year and stick to the plan.
- Host masterclasses every six weeks and change them up.
- Repeat the same masterclasses for brand awareness.
- Hire a team and have them sell for you.
- Personally write to prospects in their direct messages.
- Understand that people want to know YOU.
- Understand that nobody wants to know about you, it's about THEM.
- Start with a low ticket offer like a membership.
- Never sell low ticket. High ticket only.
- Over-deliver and ensure your clients feel special.
- Stay removed unless they pay to have proximity to you.
- Post on social media every day. No, multiple times a day. On every platform.
- Get in front of other people's audiences to grow yours.
- You don't need a big audience, you just need to nurture the one you have.
- Know your brand pillars and never deviate in your messaging.

Even writing this tip-of-the-iceberg list of contradictory advice is exhausting me! Imagine living it! But until I started questioning these rules, I thought they were needed for success. So, I scrambled. I hustled. I did as many of the things as I could, ignoring how contracted and cringy I felt inside as I kept trying to keep up with this invisible moving target.

Take the "masterclass every six weeks" launch advice for example. I would host these week-long online masterclasses multiple times a year, which would involve intricate sub-lists of rules that always seemed to be "the most important detail." People often think that the work of putting on a masterclass is sharing content to the live audience on the other side of the screen. That is, in fact, the easiest, most enjoyable part. The work part is in the naming, branding, and visual elements such as banners and promotional material. It was in the creation of the content that I would teach. It was the social media posting so the right people would want to sign up. In sending out emails leading up to the event, then daily emails during the event. And, of course, the sales sequence following the event, as well as connecting with the leads who might be interested in working with me. It is important to mention the prolonged stress of knowing that if one part is off, the whole house of cards falls.

I put myself under an enormous amount of pressure every time I ran one of these events, and my recovery would take days. I wouldn't sleep well. I would constantly be worrying about the to-do list, how many people had signed up, which details I had forgotten, and all the things that could possibly go wrong. I was a stress-case and definitely not "in my body." I was all head. And a spinning one at that.

Every time I ran a masterclass, I would experience a level of doubt in myself that is hard to write about. There was never a concern about the content—I knew that it was excellent and people always had transformational experiences. It had to do with my underlying self-doubt: *Would this be good enough for people to want to sign up to work with me?*

And I didn't trust that.

I was so busy living by other people's rules for success, I was unknowingly measuring my worth based on whether I could match the outcomes they promised. It was an intense roller coaster. Usually by midweek, I'd be a curled-up ball of exhaustion from planning and executing the masterclass, as well as experiencing crashing rejection if sign-ups were not flooding in.

If sign-ups were low, I was riddled with shame, as I saw it as a personal flaw. The way I was viewing it was that the launch didn't fail, I was the failure. This perspective was exaggerated in me because I had a team working with me—a team I was paying based on commissions of sales. So, if there were low sign-ups, there was not much money for this team who also had been working around the clock. I felt so much stress, which I ended up passing on to my team, encouraging them to keep going. I felt like a drill sergeant. This was the identity of someone in pure lack mentality, not the abundant, regulated, resourced entrepreneur I wanted to be.

I remember it all came to a head for me in this one masterclass during the black hole of the early part of the pandemic. Everyone was worried about how long this lockdown was going to be. The fear of an unknown future had become more intense, businesses couldn't hold on, relationships were suffering, families were arguing, and what had initially felt like an emergency had turned into a season of enduring. People were over the initial shock and were looking for coaching support during these rocky times that were not going away.

I already had my online business flowing for a few years at that point. I was already helping women with their mindset, tapping into new ways of thinking and new ways of understanding themselves and what was possible. So, I just leaned in to be of even more service.

During this particular masterclass, everything lined up. The topic and my messaging and delivery were all on point. My readiness to receive them into my program was on point. No masterclass had ever felt so good. I was on top of my game. The words were just pouring out of me, and the participants were taking those ideas and having breakthrough after breakthrough. The team was active and nurturing these wonderful women, and the sessions ran like honey. People were telling their friends to come and check it out, so the numbers grew every day. Sales were flooding in. They just wanted more of what we were doing together, and I had just the transformation process they were looking for. I was hitting my sales targets so easily, I could hardly believe it. A multiple six-figure launch was something I'd been holding in my mind's eye, and here it was. It was working! I was successful!

You'd think I would have been ecstatic, but I ended up in the same fetal position as when sales were low. Toward the end of the week, even though the results were incredible, I would get off the calls and immediately lie down on my sofa, feeling utterly depleted—the same depletion I felt during the losses. I thought, *What's going on? Isn't this what I am working for?*

It just didn't make me feel the way I thought it would. Or the way all those business gurus said that it would. It was confusing because although I was grateful for the financial abundance, something felt off. It was after the Day 5 call in that masterclass that it hit me: "It's a trap. There is no winning in this game." I pulled out my journal and recorded the realization that underneath all of these wins and losses is the same thread line of me using external factors to determine my worthiness. And whenever I do that, I give my power away. **When I give my power away, I do not feel successful.**

I knew I had to stop using these metrics for success, right then and there. I decided I was no longer willing to live according to the ups and downs of external validation. It was coming at too high of a cost on my well-being. It was clear now that as long as I was equating my worth with the success of my business, I was not sovereign. As long as I was chasing results as a reflection of me, I was imprisoned. And that is no way to live.

It was taking a toll on my happiness, my health, my energy, my creativity, and my desire to run a business at all. Either I changed the game or I had to get out of it. Staying and operating this way was no longer an option. Upon reflection, it's clear to me that my behaviour came from an identity created in childhood. You know, the little girl who is rewarded for doing well in school and works for positive feedback. Thinking she's a good girl when she gets that pat on the back. She matured into a proper people pleaser, always wanting to make others happy so that the validation would continue. I got very good at following the rules of others and putting their needs first.

It has always been an exhausting way to live. Prioritizing the opinions of others and measuring myself based on the outcomes is shaky ground that takes a lot of energy to maintain. So, I drew the line that day. I declared completion on the old cycle of leaning on external rules and validation to create my business, and my life, and my worth. And I started to ask questions to lead me to my new identity:

- Who do I want to be now?
- What would I absolutely love?
- How do I want to feel about myself at the end of the day?
- What does success feel like for me in this new identity?
- What changes when I live as this new version?

From that last question, I knew the gateway was to write my own rules for business and my own terms for success. I needed to author a whole new operating system. I began to imagine a reality where I was promoting my services from a genuine place of sharing. From wanting people to know about what was available and not trying to get something from them or get them to do anything. **When I shared about my services, I started thinking of them as simple invitations.** It stopped affecting me personally if they said no or if they said yes. I could see that it wasn't about me. I began sharing on social media without any objective at all. No twisty-turny manipulations or motivations.

With these authentic changes, I started to feel successful, regardless of whether money was pouring in or not. I live from the knowledge and embodiment that I am inherently worthy—because I exist. I do not need to prove it to anyone, especially myself.

Now when I see the rules of others in the industry, I am wary of any language that promotes "the only way" to do something, or language that emphasizes that one strategy is dead while another is the future. Instead, I think about where I want to go, the business values that I run with, and the lifestyle that I want to live. And I ask myself: *How does this feel for me?*

In my exploration of according to my own terms, I have discovered that my business is most successful when it is run my way. The identity I built knows that none of my business results come from an external strategy. **My new definition of success is the answers to these questions: How much am I enjoying what I do? How much am I living in an expanded state?**

It is all about how I show up for myself and then how I show up for my business. My energy dictates how aligned I am, then how powerfully and effectively I can care for my clients and their transformations from that place.

I have an entirely new set of beliefs that have led to my self-created rules. Some of them include:

- I have the most success when I am excited about my offers. My inspiration is my key.
- My masterclasses are life-changing and worthwhile, regardless of whether people sign up to work with me or not.
- I am only looking for the people who are looking for me.
- This work is my life's purpose and I live it out every time I share it.
- My energy is my superpower. The more I tend to me, the more magnetic I am.
- There is nothing more important than tending to the truth in my heart, and trusting it, every single step of the way.
- I am not here to follow other people's rules.

And in this new, aligned life where I get to truly be who I want, run the business the way I want, create offers that inspire me as I want, and model permission for others to do things their own way too, I get to live a very successful business.

And I start my day at noon.

Eight

NINA RUELENS

DEDICATION

To the future version of myself, may I continue to share my story and trust what flows through me.

To you, reading this, I hope this chapter leaves you feeling nourished, supported, and ready to choose yourself. I've got you.

And to this community of extraordinary authors and Amanda and her team, thank you for reminding me how powerful it is to be supported, seen, and not judged. The process of this would not have been as enJOYable or nearly as easy without you. It's one I will carry with me.

NINA RUELENS

Nina Ruelens is the owner of Chef Nina's Creative Kitchen, Nourish Studios, and the dog-friendly community café BE Café & Barkery in Hamilton. She guides busy, health-conscious people, especially those navigating food sensitivities, to build a personalized way of eating that works for their body and their life.

Through her BE Nourished Method, Nina offers a simple, supportive approach that helps people break old patterns, feel confident in their choices, and follow through without overthinking.

With more than twenty-five years as a chef in commercial kitchens, she has developed practical systems that make nourishing food feel simple, realistic, and sustainable, even in the busiest seasons of life. After years of burnout in the food industry, Nina began looking beyond the plate, rebuilding her health through food, awareness, and supportive practices that helped her reconnect to herself and her body. She believes nourishment is not about perfection but about building a relationship with your body that evolves with you. Her work is rooted in real life, helping people create simple systems so they can feel good in their bodies and stay consistent without overthinking it, because that's where real nourishment begins.

When she's not in the kitchen, Nina can be found with her dog, out on the water paddleboarding, or in a yoga class continuing to live the practices she shares.

Connect with Nina at **chefninaruelens@gmail.com**

MY PATH TO A MORE NOURISHED LIFE

There is a lot of noise and confusion when it comes to how to feed and fuel ourselves.

Like so many, I got very caught up in diet culture and started every fad to lose weight or look a certain way along the way, but nothing stuck or felt like it would be sustainable for me until I took real food to nourish myself. Most people think "successful" nutrition has a label: keto, vegan, gluten free, paleo. Or some think it involves measuring and counting all our calories. And as much as I did all those things, it's not what I did to lose the weight I did or get rid of the list of unhealthy symptoms I had.

I had been a chef for about five years the first time I noticed I was overweight and unwell. I had grown up as the tall and skinny girl who could eat anything I wanted. But fast-forward to working long days in a hot kitchen in the food service industry combined with its toxic lifestyle, and I gained about fifty pounds over my ideal body weight. I also had metabolic symptoms like nausea, acne, heartburn, canker sores, rashes, PMS . . . and the list goes on.

The thing is, I was always pretty active. I was running competitively and working out. But the weight and feelings of being unwell were like a roller coaster. I would hear and read about all the different diets and ways to get "healthy," and some I just couldn't get on board with. I remember one from my early stages included counting calories in ingredients like olive oil, something most, including my Italian girl roots, would say is healthy. So, I couldn't see how I was going to stick to a lifestyle of believing I had to limit these types of real-food ingredients.

The funny thing about this is I didn't actually know how unwell I was or how much weight I had gained. I thought I carried my weight pretty well, but getting ready to go out was always a struggle. Finding clothes that fell a certain way and covered what I wanted to hide added real stress in my life. I'd often end up in tears, sometimes even cancelling plans to go out. I had reached a size 16 in clothes, and my inner dialogue was not kind. But outwardly, I'd deflect with humour. I'd laugh it off and just buy a size bigger until I had to switch to plus-size shops. Even then, I'd joke that I was wearing the smallest size in Addition Elle.

How I treated my body when I was chasing weight loss was to chase extreme diets and extreme fitness. If I didn't lose enough weight, it went on the competition board with my sister and my (ex)husband. The three of us had turned weight loss into a running challenge. We tracked pounds lost on a board each week and whoever didn't hit the number owed the others a punishment workout. Most of the time that meant the mountain stairs: ten rounds up and down. At the time, it felt like motivation. Looking back, though, it was just another way I was punishing my body instead of learning how to nourish it.

I'd tell myself I could eat whatever I wanted (cheesy carbs like pizza, etc.) as long as I continued to work out, but the truth was, my eating habits were not great. I can't tell you how many times I walked across the street from my bistro to get that Ruffles jar of nacho dip or ranch. I was surrounded by convenience food at the golf course where I worked, so having a Snickers daily was a thing. I saw it the same as a protein bar in many ways. And when I worked long days and felt too busy to eat a proper meal, I'd snack mindlessly until I could finally binge on the buffet. I remember nights when I had cooked beautiful meals for hundreds of people: the salads were fresh, the vegetables perfectly roasted, and the plates going out looked incredible. I made sure everyone else was taken care of first. The guests were happy, the team was fed, the service was running smoothly. And then I would look down at my own plate at the end of the night. Most of the time it wasn't a nourishing meal at all. It was filled with all the pastas, carbs, and sweets I craved.

I was very good at nourishing everyone else. I just hadn't learned how to nourish myself yet.

And even when I transitioned to my restaurant, I would regularly do a full plate of mashed potatoes and blue cheese sauce that was meant as a side for the beef tenderloin. Yes, I know it all sounds delicious. And it really, really was, which is what made it so, so hard to resist!

I didn't realize how much this approach was costing me physically, mentally, and emotionally. I had a long list of unwellnesses that I had come to normalize. One day, while bending over to tie my shoes, I couldn't breathe properly and my face felt pressure. I thought, *Yikes. I have been ignoring this for a while and pretending like it's okay.* I decided then to finally pay attention and take things a little more seriously.

I had heartburn daily. My dad even said to me, "You know that's not good for you. You should probably get that checked out." So, I went to the doctor and she put me on medication. It worked for a while. And then it didn't. I went back and got more medication. She said the next time we'd have to do a scope down my throat.

I had severe back pain that eventually led to surgery for an L4–L5 herniated disc causing sciatica. I used to set an alarm thirty minutes before I actually needed to wake up so I could take a fistful of Advil and let the pills kick in before I tried to get out of bed.

I had acne every cycle and even in between them. My menstrual cramps were so brutal that they made me nauseous and sick on a regular basis. Leaving my house on the first and second day of my cycle felt almost impossible. But I'm a pusher. I don't call in sick. I don't stop. I would just take more painkillers and do what I needed to do.

I had night sweats in my twenties that sounded exactly like what women in menopause describe. I would wake up with soaked sheets, changing my clothes multiple times a night.

I was deeply disconnected from myself. Not knowing how to truly nourish myself and pushing instead of listening cost me my health, cost me my fertility, and ultimately cost me my relationships. At the time, I believed this was just the price of discipline.

One day, I was in the kitchen prepping away while a TV was on in the background with one of the morning talk shows. I heard a stat that food is responsible for 85 percent of weight loss. Something about hearing that stuck, and from then on, I focused on food more than movement for my weight loss. It made me question why I was punishing my body so much through movement while paying so little attention to how I was actually fuelling myself. I didn't have a new plan yet, I just knew the old way didn't make sense anymore. I didn't change everything at once, but I did change how I ate and how I looked at food.

I started with something called the "4 Day Diet," which was created by Dr. Ian K. Smith. What attracted me to this framework was the idea that we can do anything for four days. As a mindset technique, that really worked for me. I loved playing around with the list of detoxing foods comprised in this particular framework.

Because I was in kitchens surrounded by food, and at this time it was my own bistro kitchen, I had all the resources at my disposal to make the nourishing choices I wanted for myself. I remember thinking, *I'm a chef and food is the one thing I can actually control.* So, I started to do just that.

I got creative in making salad dressings with puréed beans, and even my sister, a very picky eater, got on board. Every time I made something she liked and I was able to get one of those nutrient-dense, healthy ingredients on her plate, it felt like a huge win.

Funny enough, I've done that with food for a long time. If I can make a mushroom hater love my mushroom soup, or make a blue cheese sauce taste amazing to someone who normally despises it, those are culinary wins for me. So, I started having fun exploring recipes and making nourishing dishes for myself and my family.

We all started losing weight. And we never felt like we were starving or missing out, which is the part I love. When healthy food tastes delicious, everything changes.

This worked. I could still eat food I enjoyed and lose weight. It felt sustainable, like something I could actually keep doing long term as a lifestyle. The food changes worked, but they were not the reason the weight stayed off.

In fact, I have let the scale go back up twice since my first big loss. Stress from life creeps in. I also got really comfortable in a relationship, started eating out a lot, and old patterns came back. I was living pretty unaware, still disconnected and not fully understanding that food is an actual addiction. It serves us emotionally in so many ways, both as a crutch and as a way to celebrate. Think about any family gathering or party: there's always food involved. And no one wants to be the weirdo who says no to birthday cake.

But for me, letting myself have a little became a habit. Then I'd have a little more, and before long, the whole cake was gone. It wasn't until I started discovering my own patterns, learning which foods actually support my own unique system, then choosing me and only me from a place of love and understanding, that things began to change.

I know a lot of people make choices based on the fact that they have to get up every morning and clothe and feed their kids regardless of how they feel. I hear many people say they make healthy choices to have the energy for their kids. I don't have kids, but I still want the energy so I can show up for my nephew and my family. I want to be the fun young aunt with the vitality to keep up.

But ultimately, I had to do this for me. I had to ask myself what would truly nourish me, what would make me feel good, because I am the only one who is going to do this for myself.

This is where choosing myself finally came in. Not perfectly, but intentionally. I realized no one was coming to save me. If I wanted to feel good in my body, I had to be the one asking what would support me and actually make my life feel better. Choosing myself is the part I had to grow into, and it's why the weight stays off now.

Choosing myself wasn't a big declaration, it was a series of small, daily decisions.

There are certain foods now that I say no to, simply because the cost doesn't outweigh the gain. I ask myself, Will this nourish me? That question alone has changed everything for me. We're wired to want the reward, even when we know the consequence. I lived that way for a long time. Nothing truly shifted until I learned to love myself enough to not want to live that way anymore.

One practical change for me was surrounding myself with nourishing food. I once heard that a sign of addiction is not being able to say no when something is around. When it comes to wine and sugar, that was very real for me. **So, instead of relying on willpower, I started keeping better options around, making supportive choices easier, and being honest about what didn't serve me.**

I also began swapping things out. Going to a yoga class became my new night out instead of going to a bar. Movement with breath helped me reconnect to my body and actually notice how things felt. As for competitive running, I still love it, I just do it differently now and with the wisdom of my body. So, that might mean no music or going slower. I stay present as much as I can through most movements to focus on my posture and what my body is saying to me.

Paying attention to my mood was huge. Alcohol was obvious. It would make me feel hot, overly confident, then eventually off. But noticing how certain foods affected my mood surprised me just as much. Gluten, for example, would leave me feeling lethargic and unmotivated, almost disconnected from myself, so now I make conscious choices based on how I know things will make me feel and whether it's worth feeling that way. And if I am in a true place of love for myself, I make the nourishing choices that will support my body and not deplete it.

Choosing myself now looks like awareness. It looks like making decisions based on how I want to feel, not just what I want in the moment. These aren't rigid rules, they're supportive choices that help me stay in relationship with my body and my life.

I used to think weight loss and being healthy required punishment, shame, and guilt when we messed up. That's how I approached it for years. And now, the way I look at nutrition couldn't be further from that.

That approach might work for a short period of time, but real sustainability and a true lifestyle shift require more than force. What actually worked for me was planning ahead—not out of restriction, but out of care. I plan for my future self. I think about Nina during the week and what she's going to eat so she doesn't end up scrounging, exhausted, or pulling into a drive-thru because there are no better options available. Having a loose plan for the week removes so much stress and decision fatigue. Tracking everything I ate or counting calories never worked for me long term. **What did work was planning ahead and prepping a few things so**

they were ready when I needed them. That shift alone changed everything. It made nourishing myself simpler, more consistent, and something I could actually live with and share with others.

I created the BE Nourished Method for people like me. I help busy humans eat real food, feel better, and build support that actually fits their life. Rather than focusing on control or rules, we work with awareness, support, and practical tools that help rebuild trust with food, your body, and yourself.

I know firsthand how busy schedules can derail even the best intentions, so I deliver prepared food, making it as convenient as takeout. I also offer cooking and wellness reset classes and catering. My work is informed by yoga therapy and grounded in the understanding that our relationship with food is deeply connected to the nervous system, lived experience, and how safe we feel in our bodies. The delicious food we cook and the supportive classes we create are all nourishing practices I continue in my own life now.

My definition of successful nutrition used to look like counting calories and pushing myself at the gym, ignoring my symptoms or masking them with drugs or alcohol. I lived in an all-or-nothing mentality and forced my way through things instead of listening to my body.

What changed was awareness. For me, that became everything. We can't change something we aren't aware of. But even once we are aware, nothing shifts until we actually want to change.

And that was hard for me to understand for a while. I am the first person to want to help everyone else, and I had to understand that no change is possible until someone truly wants it for themselves. What brings someone to the point of saying, "I don't want to live this way anymore" looks different for everyone. I think we all have our own version of rock bottom, and some of us tolerate a lot more from ourselves than others.

For me, things changed when I no longer wanted to tolerate certain behaviours or unwellnesses in my own life. That decision came back to self-love and to the practices yoga and meditation taught me. **Weight loss is not about the shape we see in the mirror, it's about how we feel and the relationship we have with the body we're living in.**

If weight loss or finding a body you feel healthy in has never worked for you, I want you to know something. There is a lot of noise out there. New information. New diets. New rules being thrown at us all the time. It's easy to feel overwhelmed and frustrated and to try everything . . . only to feel like nothing works.

So, here is something simple you can start today. Every time you go to eat, pause and ask yourself: "Will this nourish me or deplete me?"

Is what you are choosing made with ingredients you can actually recognize and pronounce? Is it free from added sugars or sugar-type ingredients that keep you stuck in the cycle?

It breaks my heart knowing how hard people are on themselves and how often we compare our bodies and our lives to what other people are doing. In today's world, it's incredibly hard not to feel like you have to keep up or to compare what you have to what someone else has.

The truth is, you are you, and no one else is living in your body. What works for one person may not work for another, and even the reasons we want change can be very different. The more grounded we can become, the more we can truly love our own body and feel grateful for all that it does. I truly believe that when we come back to ourselves with awareness, care, and compassion, we put ourselves on the path to a more nourished life.

Nine

KAREN ARMSTRONG

DEDICATION

This chapter is dedicated first to my husband, Munro, who believed in me and supported me even when he didn't understand everything I did. I could never be all that I am without you, and I am forever grateful.

This is also for my three sons, Taylor, Eldon, and Haydon. Being your mom is still the biggest joy in my life, and you have been my greatest teachers. Wanting to do the best for you took me down paths I would not have otherwise found. And to watch you as you guide and lead your own lives, love your families, and support your friends makes my heart burst. May you always follow your hearts and be sovereign in your decisions.

Finally, to my friends, colleagues, and clients through all these years. Thank you for trusting me, challenging me, and growing with me. We have a strong and wise community. The future that I see through you holds miracles beyond what we have yet known.

KAREN ARMSTRONG

Karen Armstrong is the founder of Inside Out, where she has expressed her calling as a Reiki master, teacher, healer, and coach for the past twenty-six years. Karen has had a deep curiosity for understanding relationships from a young age, and over time, this expanded into the deeper inner relationship expressed through our mind, heart, and body. During the transition between her corporate career and self-employment, her car became a university, bringing hours of teaching through CDs of teachers like Caroline Myss, Esther and Jerry Hicks, Wayne Dyer, Russ Hudson and Don Riso, and Neil Donald Walsch, to name a few.

She is still a lifelong student, having taken courses in emotional intelligence, traditional Chinese medicine, homeopathy, energy medicine, and educational kinesiology, and she has years of study in Reiki and the Enneagram. It's always about learning that our whole being is created and interconnected to support our life's journey, if we would only listen and trust it more. All this experience comes through whether she is teaching Reiki, offering healing sessions, or hosting her monthly Women's Wellness Circle.

When she is not in her professional role, Karen's greatest joys in life come from her incredible family and her love of singing, cooking, and adventuring in nature.

Connect with Karen on Instagram **@insideout_reikilife**
or visit **www.in-side-out.com**

SEEING WHAT REALLY MATTERS

Twenty-five years ago, I left my corporate career after realizing I had become the poster child for the burned-out "Super Mom" who thought she could do it all without asking for help. I was searching for more than my hectic life was providing at the time, so I went back to school and then started my own practice offering Reiki and Enneagram relationship coaching with a tagline of "Encouraging Balance in Life," as that is what I was in search of. But even with my new course of action, I was still working from my deeply engrained belief of what success was: work hard, make things happen, rarely say no, and continue to stay on the leading edge of my new personal development path. The core of my being believed that if I was accepted and loved by the important people around me, then I was worthy.

I grew up focusing on making the people around me happy and looking for acknowledgement from what I accomplished. This need for outer approval ran so deep, and it was an impossible task with which to keep up. My version of success was still striving. I knew how to push a little harder, override a little longer, and applaud myself for endurance even when my body was quietly asking for mercy. I called it discipline. I called it commitment. I called it growth. From the outside, I totally looked like I led a successful life and there was a lot of good in it. I was just unaware of the inner cost that this version of success would have on my long-term health and well-being.

Then my vision began to change. Not metaphorically. Literally. I discovered at an annual optometrist checkup in the spring of 2021 that my eye pressure was high enough to warrant immediate treatment and a referral to a glaucoma specialist. I was in total shock!

The specialist did all the right things, provided his expertise, and told me I had done nothing wrong. I was just one of many who would age this way, and no diet or exercise program would make a difference. Just keep taking my drops, come in for regular checkups, and leave the rest to him. As someone who has built a life and livelihood around wellness, I had so many questions. No one addressed why my eyes were changing or stepped back to view the whole picture of my body and life. No one thought of asking what my body was trying to say as it blurred the edges of my life as I knew it.

This chapter is not about fixing my eyes. It is about learning how to see myself.

This shift actually began a year earlier in the spring of 2020. After the honeymoon phase of being forced to slow right down because of the pandemic, my body and inner wisdom took the opportunity to express a number of emotional things that I never gave any time and space to. I began the shutdown fully enjoying that my husband and I still had adult children living with us and we got to spend lots of time together cooking wonderful meals and working on projects on the property that had been on the to-do list for years. It was heartwarming and fun. After a couple months, the family business was deemed essential, and while their long working days resumed, mine did not.

I didn't know quite how I actually felt, but my body knew. I developed severe digestive issues and was in acute pain. I went to see my GP, and after full bloodwork, X-rays, and ultrasounds, nothing significant showed up. While that was a relief, it was also confusing.

This became my puzzle to understand. Due to the nature of my work along with my active participation in numerous business groups over the years, I am incredibly blessed to know some very talented practitioners in my circle, so it didn't take me long to figure out my next steps.

I reached out to a holistic nutritionist and was guided to do additional bloodwork along with a GI Map functional test. With the results from these, I began a diet and supplement protocol to restore my gut health.

I kept up my yoga practice both online at home and in-person at a friend's place. I also walked almost every day with my dog and a couple close friends.

And for my mind (but really my heart), I began working with a personal coach, another colleague whom I had known in my area for years. She guided me through some big questions and taught me how to lean into what was arising with curiosity and compassion. That was not an easy space to embrace for myself, and I shed buckets of tears as those tender places were touched inside me. Laura helped me quiet my mind to allow my heart to take up more space. It was not easy for me to release control, as guarding my vulnerable inner truth had always made me feel safe.

By November 2021, I accepted the nudge from my coach and decided to take a sabbatical. It took me four months to step into it from the time I made the decision that it was a good idea. Each month would arrive and I'd talk myself out of it being the "right" time. I still had clients to see and commitments to fulfill. In mid-November, I got sick and had to cancel everything for the week. After spending two days in bed, I could not sleep on the third night. At 1 a.m., I made some tea, grabbed my journal, and started writing. I asked my body: Why now? What was it stopping me for? The answer suddenly landed in my awareness: I had made a promise to go on sabbatical and take a pause and I kept making excuses and delaying it. I knew this was my truth, so I made a new promise that I would send a newsletter out the next day to announce my decision. I slept deeply for the rest of the night and started feeling my body healing after I sent the newsletter out.

I did not know how long my sabbatical would be, however, as we had our first grandchild arriving and two of our three sons' weddings planned for 2022, and I wanted to be totally present for all of it.

This is what I wrote in my journal on February 21, 2021:

I am being called to invest more in my soul's growth by spending more time listening and tuning into me. By investing in this support system called Roots. By accepting that it's time to stand up for and take action on what is important to me. Time seems urgent to let go of fear and move forward.

I am ready to keep this growth going and moving forward. To feel and know my infinite power through love, to make the biggest difference I can by who I can be for me and the greater unfolding.

One way I can be more compassionate with myself would be to invite more humour.

It was fascinating to read this entry later that year after I finally activated my decision to take a sabbatical. The seed had been planted, and although I resisted my inner nudges to take my sabbatical, life supported me to follow through. This was a very powerful turning point. It began in December and lasted until March before I began accepting a few clients who reached out to me. My official return was not until May. These months were spent learning to listen deeper to myself and asking a lot of questions. I reviewed and redefined:

My values – This process was supported by my coach. Identifying my core values greatly impacted the ease of setting my priorities. In fact, I am not sure how true priorities can be sustained if they do not support our values. Like our truth, our values will always be revealed over time in how we show up and by the choices we make.

My priorities – I started taking time to notice what brought me joy verses what created stress. When I was not conscious of my values, I would have difficulty determining what was a priority and just attempt to do it all. I wanted to please myself and please everyone else. Anyone who has been here will know that this can create many conflicting priorities, which, in turn, sets us up for disappointment.

My self-talk – I began noticing my negative thought patterns and expectations. I have always considered myself an optimistic person and did not realize how tough I was on myself. I understand now that this goes back to my childhood belief that I needed to show up a certain way to be accepted and loved. I learned that I am an optimistic person; I see the good in life, in experiences, and in people. I just had a harder time giving that grace to myself when I thought I was not measuring up.

My dreams – I pondered what dreams still wanted to be nurtured and which ones were outdated. I realized that some dreams were actually old stories that I had not taken time to sit with myself and ask if they still mattered. I let go of my original dream of renovating our home along with the many years of hurt due to unfulfilled expectations. It did not mean that I don't want to move forward with changes in our home, but once I let go of the old vision and hurts, there was room for a modified vision that fit the needs of both my husband and me now. That vision is much different than thirty years ago. The creativity and joy have room to enter the process of this new dream.

New healthy habits – By spending more time being curious about what I needed and reading/listening to numerous articles and podcasts, I incorporated some small, consistent habits, especially in the morning. I take my dog outside first thing upon rising, mostly barefoot (except for during a couple winter months), and do some deep breathwork and simple body movement before coming back into the house. Then I get my warm water and tea and meditate or journal in front of my red light. It has become a game changer in how the rest of my day unfolds. I feel grounded, fuelled, and ready to enjoy the day.

The news of my vision diagnosis affected me deeply. I would oscillate between the worst-case scenario of early blindness to trusting that if my body created this, my body could heal this. I just had to figure out what its message was to me. **"Life is showing up *for* me, not *to* me" became a helpful mantra to open my perspective to all possibilities from one of victimhood.**

After laser treatment, daily drops, and eventually glaucoma surgery in 2022, my eye pressure stubbornly hovered at the edge of "acceptable." I dove into research, podcasts, supplements, light therapies, acupuncture, and every supportive practice I could find, sensing there was a deeper message. I believed that my eyes were teaching me something. In the summer of 2024, a podcast by Gary Brecka sparked a breakthrough: He explored the link between high histamine and elevated blood pressure or eye pressure. Because I had a lifelong history of allergies, the pieces clicked. Testing revealed a gut bacterial infection disrupting my body's ability to regulate histamine. A targeted protocol brought noticeable healing, yet scar tissue required one final laser procedure. In the months that followed, my eye pressure finally settled into a healthy range.

I felt so much relief and was optimistic that I had listened and learned and healed; however, I had one more hurdle to experience. When pressure later spiked again alongside digestive symptoms, further testing uncovered a lingering infection that traced back to compromised teeth and low-grade dental infections. Addressing the dental source, along with taking supplements and focusing on dietary support, finally resolved the underlying imbalance.

My digestion stabilized, my eye pressure returned to normal, and I was able to discontinue one of the prescription drops. The struggle became a revelation: high histamine driven by hidden infection was the missing link, and by trusting my inner guidance while honouring medical care, I restored balance from the inside out. And this journey rippled into every part of my life.

Over this period of time as I was learning, healing, and tuning into my body and my heart at a deeper level than I ever had, something else shifted. In my Reiki practice, I understood that clients came to me looking for something to be different in their lives. I trusted that if I could assist them in understanding the messages their body was giving them, and if they would follow through with practices to honour and change what was not feeling right, the healing would happen. Every time! I am truly in awe of the power of our mind-body connection and how we can make positive changes if we understand the underlying issues and have the courage, patience, and support to make them.

I am not saying this is an easy journey; it was not for me. The fear of losing my sight and not being able to stop it brought me to my knees in disbelief. There were times that my thoughts went down the rabbit hole of not being able to see my grandchildren's faces as they grew up or to take in the beauty of nature and this incredible world. How could I stay in the front row of my chorus where I am able to do all the choreography or even continue to sing in this group that has been part of my life for forty years? That is what the prognosis of glaucoma looks like when you research it online. It's an inevitable steady decline of your sight.

Thankfully, I was unable to stay in that space, to stay crippled with fear. There was my underlying spirit that would not give up, that whispered to me to listen deeper to my body. My eyes were messaging me that something was out of alignment in my beingness, and as I softened into this and began to stay more open, more information showed up for me on my searches.

It started with learning about the positive impacts of taking in natural light, doing eye exercises, and learning what foods, supplements, castor oil, and even essential oils can do to support our vision. And at the same time with my coaching support, I was going deeper into asking myself questions about how I saw my life and really, how I saw myself. Coming from a young person who had learned to see myself from the messages I received from others to really looking at and seeing myself has been the biggest part of this whole journey so far. The lines between what I feel I should do, the picture I created on how to be a good, caring, and loving person, and what I naturally want to do become subtle. They are often the same with different energy behind them. The feeling of expectation verses desire.

I thoroughly enjoy being of service; it fills my cup and my heart. However, if the focus is always outward, then my cup gets depleted. It was time to include myself in the picture of who I look after and I am slowly learning that if I put "me" first, I have all the energy in the world available to be there for others.

My sabbatical taught me that. I felt the deep nudge that I was being called to do my work differently, but if I was always too busy to pause and listen to the calling of my heart song, nothing was going to change. I would get more frustrated. I did a lot of self-care on my sabbatical and felt such joy preparing our gardens and property for the wedding we would be hosting. I was calmer yet energized and in a lovely flow. When I had a few clients message me for appointments four months into my sabbatical, it felt right to say yes. I did not announce my arrival back; instead, there was a slow, steady increase in the hours I worked. I had no great download or epiphany of great changes. What I did realize is that I had changed. My presence was greater, my intuition was deeper, and the shifts taking place for clients were bigger. The more I learn, the more I can share, and I know that will never stop. The difference is that I do not have to always seek it out, believing the next piece of knowledge will make me better. As I relax into the flow of life, what I am meant to learn and experience will find me. That is a rich gift to bring into my practice.

When I paused and did less, I became more. More of who I truly am, not what I was trying to be. Then my eyes and body had a window to speak to the deeper levels of healing required. My eyes taught me how to see myself.

Looking back now, I can see that my health did not interrupt my life so much as it highlighted a belief program that began decades earlier. The striving, the search for approval, the belief that worth was something to be earned, all found their expression in my body that asked to be honoured rather than driven. My eyesight became the invitation I could no longer ignore. It asked me to trust myself, to say no without justification, and to accept that love does not require performance. The two values that have always lived at the core of my soul carried me through this redefinition. **Love, given time and attention, truly can change everything.** And not giving up, I discovered, does not always mean pushing forward. **Sometimes it means staying present, listening deeply, and allowing success to look like acceptance, wholeness, and finally coming home to love myself.**

Ten

BRITTANY MILLER

DEDICATION

This is dedicated to my family: Grayson, Thalia, Raiyah, Rhett, Luca, Orion, and our upcoming twins. My beautiful, unique kiddos, you all inspire me daily, encouraging me to slow down and try new things. You are the reason I get out of bed and the passion behind all my business ideas. I hope you know how much I love you, and that I do this to inspire you to live a joyous, limitless life.

This chapter comes from the love and support of my incredible fiancé, Grayson, whose continued encouragement makes me forever grateful. He is my sounding board, my rock that keeps me grounded, and the reason I get to chase a never-ending stream of dreams. Thank you for believing in this vision with me and supporting the life we're creating together—one that blends ambition, freedom, and family in a way that feels aligned for us.

Lastly, thank you to my parents and my mother-in-law for loving us all unconditionally and being the support system we need for our growing family and business.

BRITTANY MILLER

Brittany Miller is an online marketing strategist, podcast host, and the founder of Brittany Miller Socials, where she helps entrepreneurs turn marketing overwhelm into simple, sustainable strategies that actually drive sales. Brittany supports women, especially moms, who are building businesses in the margins of real life. Through social media strategy, email marketing, and podcasting, she teaches her clients how to grow their visibility, build genuine connections, and create consistent income without being online 24/7.

She is also the host of the *Go Get Great* podcast, where she blends practical marketing strategies with honest conversations about business, motherhood, and creating a business that supports your life. Brittany's work is rooted in the belief that you don't need to hustle harder or do more, you just need the right strategy. Her mission is to help business owners get seen, loved, and paid, and to build profitable, freedom-focused businesses that support their lives, not take them over.

When she's not working, you'll find Brittany navigating life as a mom, renovating her home, starting a new hobby, or dreaming up new ways to build a business that allows for more time, more presence, and more freedom.

Connect with Brittany on Instagram **@brittanymillersocials, @brittanynmiller_** or visit **www.brittanymillersocials.ca**

THROWING MY CHECKLIST OUT THE WINDOW

Standing in the public bathroom at the mall and staring at two pink lines was the start of my redefinition. This was the moment I knew my life wasn't going to unfold the way I had planned. After all, I wasn't married. I wasn't even engaged, although my partner and I had been together for a year and a half, and we'd recently purchased our first home, a cute two-bedroom fixer-upper in London, Ontario. My checklist was all out of order, even though I'd been following a certain path my entire life.

I was the first one in my family to attend university, which is something I didn't take for granted. My dad dropped out of high school to work on a farm, then transitioned to construction and had a successful career as a heavy-equipment operator, which paid well and let my mom stay home. But that came with a lot of travel and time away from our family. I could tell that a long career of manual labour was not what my parents wanted for me. So, early on, I created a vision of success that included a university degree, followed by a corporate career in heels and family life with my businessman husband and our two loving kids.

I graduated with my honours bachelor of business administration, specializing in human resources with a minor in English. At least my title sounded impressive because on a personal level, I didn't feel impressive. I was so burned out from hustling to get good grades in all my classes, working full time to cover my bills (and even still, I graduated with $40,000+ in student debt), babysitting, volunteering, and attempting to have a social life.

I was like a horse with blinders on, galloping toward what I thought I should get rather than taking a moment to question what I actually wanted. My narrow focus toward "success" didn't bring me the happiness and joy I had envisioned. I felt discontent and unease. This was my first taste of how unfulfilling it is to chase someone else's version of success. But I didn't realize that until a few years later.

The minute Thalia was born and I held her in my arms, all the goals I had and things I thought I wanted, like climbing the corporate ladder, seemed shallow and silly. All I wanted to do was spend time with her and be a good mom. I wondered whether other things on my checklist also needed to change, but I was too scared to make the changes I knew I needed to. How could I just give up on everything I spent the last twenty-five years working toward? Wouldn't that make me a failure? If I did find the courage to make a change, what would I want to change it to? Could I really be a stay-at-home mom? After all, I did love my job.

For better or worse, sometimes life happens and it forces you to make a decision, and that's exactly what happened to me in the spring of 2022. We'd now welcomed our second daughter, Raiyah, and I realized my dream of having two kids also needed changing because I didn't feel done at two. Where was the little boy I dreamed about while I was pregnant with Thalia? That was a thought for another day, though, because it was time for me to plan my return to work after my second maternity leave.

When I reached out to my boss about working from home, she informed me I would be required to return to the office at least two days a week. I was gutted. It felt like the rug was being pulled out from under my feet. I had depended on my job and the stability it brought. Even though I knew I wanted to spend more time with my kids, the thought of being unemployed riddled me with anxiety. I had a lot of debt racked up on my credit card from our second set of home renovations. What was I going to do? I needed money, but I didn't have childcare to work outside the home.

Ultimately, I was forced to resign. All I could think was *How is this happening to me?*

To really drive home the fact that I wasn't meant to stay in that job, the day I handed in my resignation letter, we found out we were expecting our third baby. I was terrified. When the girls were born, I knew I wanted to change my goals because my priorities had changed. Success no longer looked like getting the next promotion; it looked like being able to wipe tears when they fell and got an ouchie, or to tuck them into bed at night and be there in the morning when they woke up. But it took until this moment when I literally had no other options for me to actually make the change. Fear coupled with my insecurities asking "What now?" and reminding me of all the ways I'd failed before. I felt paralyzed. I didn't realize this wasn't happening *to* me, it was happening *for* me.

Being backed into a corner made me take a deep breath and jump, praying that what was on the other side of quitting my job would be good for my family and me. And it was. Looking back now, I'm so grateful for this moment because without it, I would have continued listening to the negative voice in my head and stayed in that safe, secure job. The one that would have kept me away from my kids all day, which wasn't what I wanted. In reality, this decision to leave my job (while not the right option for everyone) had been there this whole time, I had just been too afraid to give up on my checklist and my current way of living that wasn't serving me.

This was how I accidentally started to redefine success. Being jobless with a mortgage to pay and kids to feed is one heck of a motivator. I had started Brittany Miller Socials as a hobby project a few months before because I was dying to talk to anyone other than my toddlers during the pandemic and figured it would be easier to give that a go full time than start something new. And I figured I already had a few clients so I must be decent at it, right? I wasn't set on running a social media management business, but a colleague told me I'd be good at it and that many business owners needed the skillset I had. Since I needed the money, I figured, why not?

In the beginning, it wasn't easy. Going from "this is fun/extra money" to "I really need this income," it was easy to fall into the habit of trying to work 24/7. Which, if you have kids, is a recipe for frustration and burnout. Moms don't get a traditional nine-to-five workday. I started getting up before my kids and created a morning routine that gave me the energy to be productive all day. I'd start with a workout, have a shower, get dressed for the day, then do some journalling or light work while I ate breakfast. By then, the kids were usually awake, so I'd make them breakfast and we'd play for a bit until nap time when I'd pull my computer out again to work for an hour or two before lunch and afternoon playtime. By then, Grayson would usually be awake (he was working nights at the time) and would play with the kids for a bit while I did a quick cleanup or a load of laundry and then retreat to my office for an hour to work some more. After that, we'd eat dinner and get the kids to bed and I'd open my computer yet again to work more. I often ended up falling asleep at my desk around ten or eleven at night, only to wake up the next day and do it all over.

It was the exact opposite of glamorous, but it worked. I was a burned-out mess but financially, we managed to get by.

That "take a leap of faith because you don't have a choice and your back is to the wall" moment taught me a very valuable lesson. I can do it. It taught me that the voice inside doesn't define who I am or what I can do. **Changing my definition of success and**

throwing my checklist out the window doesn't mean I failed. I can be a present mom and a business owner.

I learned that "failing" doesn't mean failing, it means learning. And from that, I started to take small steps away from the life I thought I wanted and move toward what I actually do want. It took longer to figure out than I thought it would, and it's a definition that changes depending on the season of life I'm in.

When I first handed in my resignation and started focusing on my business, I didn't know where I wanted to go with it. I was solely focused on making money to keep a roof over our head and food on the table. But eventually, as I started to make money, I began taking those little steps toward a less stressful financial situation and better work-life balance. I started going to bed earlier, not needing to work until late at night to get everything done, and I stopped panicking that my card would get declined when I went grocery shopping. I wasn't taking fancy trips, but I was happy that I could pay my bills and still spend time with my kids every day. Every time I took on new clients, I had the confidence to set a new boundary, which looked like not taking client calls on Friday, then it looked like raising my prices and saying no to clients I didn't want to work with. It meant skipping takeout a few nights a month to give myself money to invest in my business and stopping offering services that I didn't enjoy doing. It meant learning to do things that felt scary and developing skills I never knew I needed to grow into the individual I needed to be to bring my new vision of success to life. It meant learning to garden and accepting that I need to be a beginner to learn new things, which may result in failure, and that's okay.

It's been a slow journey over the last four years. The path to doing this is not straight in the least. Many times I've tried things and realized they're not what I actually want, so I have to go back and readjust. **But the more you practise and learn to say no to the definitions of success that are not yours, the easier it is to say yes to the things that are.** It's a constant process of asking yourself what you want, evaluating what you have and if it brings you joy, and seeing what adjustments can be made to move you one step closer to where you want to go at that moment.

This isn't an easy process; in fact, a lot of these epiphanies came after an extensive period of burnout in my business. You'd think after wanting to be an entrepreneur for so long I would be over the moon to have my own business, and I am for the most part, but there are elements of it I don't love (like any job).

I learned to focus on what I loved and was good at and delegate the other parts:

- Staring at numbers is a surefire way to put me to sleep. So, I hired an accountant.
- I have a love-hate relationship with SEO. I love when it works and my dream clients find me, but I hate actually doing it, so I have help with that now too.
- I found audio and video editing tedious and time-consuming, so my partner stepped in to take that off my plate since he's skilled at both. That's the only reason I was able to start podcasting without falling behind on my other responsibilities and client work.

I've also experienced extended periods of burnout from working far too much for far too little, which forced me to stop and evaluate what brings me joy. I did—and continue to do—a time audit to select prices that accurately represent my time investment and the transformation my clients receive. Charging more allowed me to work fewer hours while maintaining the revenue numbers I needed for our family so I could eventually transition out of burnout into a more balanced work schedule.

This prolonged state of burnout stretched until several months after the birth of my fourth baby, Luca. We were on a vacation at a cottage in Kincardine, Ontario. It was the most relaxing and clarifying week I'd had in a long time. There's something about the sound of the water that is both soothing and empowering. While I sat on the patio watching my kids play in the sand, listening to the waves crashing in the background, the overwhelm and stress started fading away. Until it was time to leave. The closer we got to returning to our house, the tighter the muscles in my body became. By the time we made it back to the city, my body was already in fight-or-flight mode. I knew something had to give. The city felt loud, chaotic, and so busy it made my heart race. And not in a good way. I realized then that I didn't want to live like that anymore, and I didn't want my kids to grow up experiencing the same thing.

The next day, I tore my vision board off my wall and lit it on fire, watching my dreams literally go up in smoke. It was surprisingly cathartic. I cried my way through a forty-five-minute podcast episode (if you don't believe me, tune into Episode 60) that was more like a therapy session. I talked about expectations killing my joy and then cleared space to figure out what all of this meant and what I was going to do about it.

A week later, I had a plan and went after it like my life depended on it, and it kinda did. I started creating courses to help other small business owners succeed based on what I'd learned, which provided residual income. And I began offering 1:1 support for those who wanted more personal coaching support. I also publicly announced that I was cancelling my biggest revenue generator, my social media management service. I started embodying my childhood dream of being a teacher, I just wasn't doing it in a traditional classroom setting. This was another moment where I was terrified, but this leap of faith felt a little bit easier because I had already done it once when I quit my job and decided to work full time in Brittany Miller Socials. Because that turned out okay, I felt slightly more confident pivoting in my already successful business.

Not long after, I called a realtor and announced to my partner that we were selling our house to find one in the country. Thankfully, he was fully supportive. It was another scary decision from a girl who has only ever known city life and the convenience of having everything you could need within ten minutes. But every time we would leave the city, I felt called to the country. And I knew no matter how crazy the decision sounded to everyone else, I knew it was the right decision for us.

The fear, the doubt, the worried voice were all there throughout this entire process, but what surprised me more was the confidence that was prevalent in our decision to sell our former two-bedroom house and take a big, scary leap toward a slower pace of life by buying a large, two-acre, five-bedroom house in the country over an hour away from the life we had built so far.

Every little decision I had made from the time I had Thalia to now gave me the proof I needed to thank the loud, doubtful voice in my head for trying to keep me safe but also remind it that I had a proven track record of making it work and doing things differently. I was the first in my family to graduate from university; I started my own business, which now supports my family; I'm successfully navigating being a mom of five; we've fully renovated two (almost three) houses, both of which we've sold at a profit; and many more small things in-between.

I don't need to have it all figured out and I don't need to be afraid of failure. I simply need to listen to my intuition and take the next best step toward what I want. I redefine success in all the little habits and actions I take every day.

Have I accomplished all the things I want to? Not yet, but it's not because I'm not successful. I haven't achieved all the things I want to because every time I achieve something new, a new goal or aspiration comes to take its place (like becoming a published author). And that's okay, it simply means I've entered a new season and unlocked a new level of success I can reach for.

Changes in your "plan for life" don't mean you've failed. You've simply redefined success so well that you have a new definition to declare and rewrite. It's important to remember that every little decision you make along your journey supports your confidence in creating the bigger picture of what success means to you.

It's an ongoing game to challenge yourself and improve, and that is the best form of success you could ever have: harnessing your ability and confidence to do just that.

Right now, what success looks like to me is having the freedom to work when I want and wherever I want, to wake up without alarm clocks, and to have nothing on the calendar. To wander barefoot through my garden on a summer's day while my kids eat berries off the bushes. To enjoy evenings around the campfire and endless board games in the living room. To have the house everyone wants to visit and the kids are proud to call home. To take spontaneous road trips since my husband doesn't have to work because the work I do lights me up so much and provides for our family. And right now, we're building the house that will bring these dreams and this current definition of success to life. My business, Brittany Miller Socials, already gives me the flexibility to have him on paternity leave and to spend his days renovating. I'm already successful in ways I hadn't dreamed were possible.

From a career perspective, younger me dreamed of having my own business. Current me has it. I achieved this by accident and then by intentional design. And it's a privilege I live in awe of every day. This is the feeling I want for you. I want to empower more women to redefine success for themselves and to go after anything and everything they want because it's more than possible. It's just a matter of time until you reach your own definition of success. This chapter is the first stepping stone to bringing that vision to life for myself and igniting the spark in others. And that's what gets me out of bed in the morning. Well, that and my five kids!

Eleven

LAURA SINCLAIR

DEDICATION

This is dedicated to Hannah and Myles, who changed the way I define success the moment I became your mom. You are the reason I believe so deeply that ambition and presence can exist in the same life, and that success should never come at the cost of what matters most. Thank you for inspiring me to build a business—and a life—with more intention, courage, and heart. You have been my greatest teachers, my deepest motivation, and my constant reminder of what truly matters.

To every woman reading this who is building something meaningful while raising the people she loves most, this is for you too. May this book remind you that success gets to look like yours.

LAURA SINCLAIR

Laura Sinclair is the founder of This Mother Means Business, an entrepreneurial community and growth ecosystem for ambitious women building businesses alongside motherhood. She is the creator of mentorship programs, live events, and strategic spaces designed to help women grow profitable businesses with more clarity, confidence, and sustainability.

With a background in marketing, entrepreneurship, and business strategy, Laura is known for helping women simplify what feels heavy, strengthen their foundations, and create businesses that support both their ambition and their real lives. She is also an angel investor and the host of the *This Mother Means Business* podcast, where she shares honest conversations about business growth, identity, and building success on your own terms.

When she's not mentoring entrepreneurs or creating new opportunities for women in business, you'll likely find her with her family in Ontario, recording a podcast episode, or dreaming up the next big idea that helps women rise.

Connect with Laura on Instagram **@itslaurasinclair**
or visit **www.thismothermeansbusiness.com**

THE WALL I WALKED AWAY FROM

The thing I remember most about my childhood home isn't the living room or the kitchen or even my bedroom.

It is a hallway.

A long, narrow stretch of wall lined with certificates, laminated awards, merit plaques, and academic honour badges. I used to joke and call it the *Wall of Shame*, but it wasn't actually shameful at all. It was the opposite. It was the place where our achievements lived, where our worthiness was displayed, and where my childhood identity was curated like an exhibit.

And I loved that wall. I loved everything it said about me. I loved that when people walked past it, they would pause and say, "Wow, Laura. Look at all these accomplishments."

I took pride—maybe too much—in being the kid who earned the most spots on that wall. In being the one who could point and say, "That one's mine. And that. And that. And that."

I didn't know it back then, but the Wall of Shame taught me something that would take me decades to unlearn: that achievement equals worth. I felt like if I was winning, I was worthy. If I was collecting gold stars, I was safe. And if I was performing well, I was loved.

I don't blame my parents for this. They were proud, and they wanted us to thrive. The wall wasn't intentionally built as a scoreboard, but I interpreted it that way. I absorbed the idea that I needed to earn approval, that being enough was conditional, and that there was always someone watching, evaluating, and tallying.

The thing about childhood beliefs like these is, they don't often stay in childhood. This isn't a Tooth Fairy or Santa Claus–type of belief. It's the kind that grows and matures with you and hides itself inside the choices you make and the rules you follow and the life you build without ever asking whether you built it intentionally.

Despite leaving home at seventeen, I was thirty before I realized how much of my identity had been shaped by that hallway.

My mom used to tell me I came into the world asking questions. I challenged almost everything, questioned why things were the way they were, and wanted to know every answer to every question I could think to ask. I was spunky, and bold, and loved playing sports (and not just because it ended up giving me awards for the wall).

When I was ten, after years of asking my mom to let me try out for the rep soccer team, I didn't make it. I remember it felt like the end of the world. I was *just as* good at soccer as the other kids, but for some reason, I wasn't selected. As I sat on my bed with tears in my eyes, my mother looked at me and told me something I didn't fully understand until much later.

"When the coach says, 'Jump!' those kids say, 'How high?' You ask, 'Why?'"

What my mom was really saying at that moment was that I didn't fit easily into systems that rewarded blind obedience. At ten years old, I didn't care much about what this meant, I just wanted to be the kid who made the team. As an adult, however, this would come back in my life with a clarity that felt almost prophetic. Even though I tried hard to be the "how high" girl for a very long time, the truth was I was never built for unquestioned scripts; I was built to challenge them.

But when your sense of worth is tied to a hallway of achievements, you learn quickly which version of yourself gets rewarded, and which one gets inconvenient. So, I learned to turn off the "why," or at least quiet it. I learned to follow rules. I learned to perform. And I learned that if I kept performing well enough, life would keep rewarding me.

My twenties were a case study in following the program: good grades, good university, good internship, good job at a globally recognized brand, good benefits, good salary, good performance reviews. Everything I'd been raised to believe about success pointed me in one direction: stability, security, respectability, predictability. Growing in the company, and maybe even retiring from it.

For a while, I felt proud of myself. I'd look around my office—the glass walls, the polished floors, the corporate branding—and think, *I did it. I'm here. I'm one of the people who get to have this life.* But under the surface, something was off. I almost always felt empty. I had subscribed to what was prescribed to me in the halls of my childhood home, but it wasn't enough. I started questioning everything. Was this really it? Was this the life I worked so hard to achieve? Was this what success was supposed to feel like?

The truth was hard to admit: I was miserable. Not dramatically miserable, but quietly, steadily, existentially miserable. **I felt like I was living *slightly adjacent* to my own life. Close enough to pretend it was fine, but far enough that I could sense the distance.**

And once you sense that distance, it becomes very hard to ignore.

The turning point didn't happen dramatically. I walked through the door of my condo in Toronto, kicked off my heels (which I always hated wearing but insisted were required for adult success), dropped my work bag, and said to my boyfriend at the time, "I just wish I could leave all of this and run a gym."

It came out of nowhere. It wasn't a plan. It wasn't a dream I'd nurtured quietly. I had no experience that would justify it, but I knew I really liked sports and really hated going to the office every day. The gym was one of my favourite places, so owning one must be fun too!

I didn't know much at that moment, but I knew that life had to be different than *this*. That despite the reality that I was checking every box and adding to the metaphorical hallway in my mind, it wasn't fulfilling, at all. Everyone in my world thought I would be crazy to walk away from my "good job" I'd worked so hard to achieve to do something as silly as run a gym.

The gym didn't come next—not yet. The first leap was even more unexpected. I left my corporate job to help a friend I met at the gym build a nutrition coaching business. People *really* didn't understand how I could walk away from stability for a start-up. But I was walking away from a life that someone else decided I was supposed to live and blindly agreed to. I didn't need it to make sense to anyone else. I needed to be able to breathe. And for the first time, I could.

The nutrition business grew quickly in the way start-ups sometimes do: unexpectedly fast, with a current that pulls you along whether you're ready or not. On the outside, it looked like I had leapt into the dream of entrepreneurship with perfect timing. The income was the highest I'd ever earned, the clients rolled in, and the opportunities stacked up so fast that I barely had time to process anything before the next demand appeared.

I would open my laptop in the morning and the messages would already be waiting: client check-ins, sales inquiries, nutrition plans to revise, fires to put out. It became normal for my phone to buzz late into the evening, long after I should've been asleep. There was always another crisis, another expectation, another thing that felt urgent—even when it wasn't. My body lived in a constant state of tension, as if I was bracing for impact twenty-four hours a day. This was supposed to be the chapter where I felt proud, where I proved myself, where I showed everyone that I had made the right decision by leaving corporate. Instead, it became the chapter where my anxiety followed me from room to room. I didn't know how to rest. I didn't know how to say no. I didn't know how to build something without losing myself inside it.

While building the business, I got married (to someone other than that previously mentioned boyfriend), and in the stress of trying to start a family, while meeting the ever-increasing demands of the start-up and its founder, I miscarried. Twice.

The first miscarriage was hard, but the second one broke me. I had just returned from a three-day "retreat" with the nutrition company's executive team, landed at Pearson Airport in Toronto, and immediately started miscarrying. I remember sitting on the bathroom floor, feeling the weight of grief mixed with a quiet, shameful truth: stress had played a role. I knew my body had been running on fumes and I'd ignored every sign it tried to give me. And underneath all the pain was a deeper realization I didn't want to face: **I had built a version of success that was actively harming me.**

That season forced me into a kind of honesty I had been avoiding for years. It showed me the true cost of a life built on performance and external validation. It made me see how deeply I had internalized the idea that pushing harder was the only way to prove my worth, even if it meant pushing myself past the point of breaking.

Walking away from that business wasn't just a brave entrepreneurial decision, it was survival. It was reclaiming my body and choosing life over achievement. I didn't yet know how to choose something different. I only knew how to run from what was destroying me (I was still the girl with the hallway, after all). So, I ran again, hoping the next chapter would heal what this one had broken. After leaving the nutrition business, I made the leap I'd once whispered out loud after a long day in corporate . . . I bought a gym.

It felt like stepping into alignment and reclaiming autonomy. It felt like beginning again, but this time on my terms. I remember picking up the keys and thinking, *This is it. This is the life I'm meant to live.*

In some ways, that was true. Owning a gym was supposed to give me freedom. Instead, I rebuilt the same patterns in new surroundings. I was still the person who woke up thinking about work and went to bed thinking I hadn't done enough. I was still the woman who thought leadership meant doing everything yourself. I was still chasing that familiar feeling of proving myself through effort, a.k.a. more effort than anyone else. The days blurred together: early mornings rolling open the garage door before the sun came up, coaching sessions back-to-back, programming workouts, managing staff, cleaning equipment, dealing with unexpected repairs, fielding member questions, updating social media, and responding to emails I never seemed to get ahead of.

By the time evening rolled around, I was still working. By the time I got home, I was depleted. And by the time my head hit the pillow, I was already thinking about what tomorrow demanded.

The gym grew. The revenue grew. The community grew. But so did the weight I carried, the pressure I felt, and the quiet whisper that I was losing myself again. And I kept telling myself, *It's fine. This is what entrepreneurship takes.* But it wasn't the gym that was the problem. It was the version of myself I kept forcing into every chapter.

Then, after a year of owning the gym, I became a mother. And motherhood left no space for illusions. It is impossible to keep living on autopilot once you're responsible for a tiny human who mirrors your energy, your pace, and your presence (or lack thereof). Motherhood shined a spotlight on the parts of my life I'd been able to ignore until then: the overworking, the constant stress, the way I allowed my business to swallow my identity.

I wanted to be present, to be engaged. I wanted to feel like I was actually *there* for the moments that mattered instead of constantly rushing through them with one foot already planted in work. **But wanting something and being able to access it are two very different things.**

At that point in my life, my family wasn't getting the best of me. They were getting whatever remained after my business took priority. I loved them deeply, but love alone doesn't create presence. Space does. And I didn't have any. If I'm honest, I don't think I would have stopped on my own. I had already proven, more than once, that even when something wasn't working, I could push through it. I was good at enduring and convincing myself that discomfort was temporary and sacrifice was necessary. I could feel the misalignment, but I was fluent in ignoring it. I knew how to keep going long after my body, my energy, and my intuition were asking me to slow down.

What actually changed everything wasn't a realization, it was the pandemic. When the world shut down, my life slowed with it—not by choice, but by circumstance. The gym closed in 2020, and with it went the rhythm I had been living inside for years. The packed schedule disappeared. The constant motion stopped. The pressure I had learned to normalize finally loosened its grip.

At first, that stillness was deeply uncomfortable. Without a physical space to run, without a calendar packed from morning to night, I was left alone with questions I had avoided for a long time. There was nowhere to rush to, nowhere to hide. No external urgency to justify exhaustion. Just time, quiet, unstructured, unfamiliar time (and a newborn baby).

In that space, something shifted. For the first time, I wasn't asking how to keep going. I was asking how I actually wanted to live. How I wanted my days to feel. How I wanted work to fit into my life instead of swallowing it whole. **I stopped reacting and started reflecting.**

I didn't arrive at answers all at once. They came slowly, in fragments, in moments that felt almost ordinary. Sitting at the kitchen table without checking my phone. Being present for dinner without mentally replaying the workday. Noticing how my body felt when it wasn't bracing for the next demand.

And the question that kept returning was: How do I want to live my life?

Not how should I live it. Not how does it look from the outside. Not what would make other people proud. But how do *I* want my life to feel? That question changed everything.

One unremarkable evening, we took a hard look at the realities of owning a business during the pandemic. The numbers really weren't great, we'd lost over half our revenues, and I got to ask myself a really important question: "Do I want to rebuild this business that had nearly broken me?" When you consider my patterns previously, my answer was pretty remarkable. It was simply no.

We decided to close the gym permanently at the end of 2020. I was three months postpartum, with no income, and not a lot of certainty about what I would do next, but I did have a lifetime of scrappiness and achievement to guide me. So, I pivoted my business online and started supporting women in their marketing and business endeavours.

When I started my online business, I did it with a level of awareness I had never had before. **I wasn't just building something new, I was consciously choosing not to repeat what I already knew didn't work.**

I knew what it felt like to chase success at the cost of my health. I knew what it felt like to build a business that demanded constant sacrifice. I knew what it felt like to tie my worth to how much

I could endure. This time, I paid attention. I built slowly. Intentionally. With boundaries. I made decisions based not just on growth, but on sustainability. I thought carefully about how much I wanted to work, how I wanted to structure my days, and what kind of energy I wanted my business to require from me. I didn't just ask whether something would move the business forward, I asked whether it supported the life I wanted to live. And something remarkable happened.

The business grew. Not because I worked harder, but because I worked differently. It expanded without consuming me. It supported my life instead of competing with it. For the first time, success didn't feel like something I was chasing. It felt like something I was living inside of.

What surprised me most was how many women recognized themselves in this shift. They came to me accomplished, capable, and quietly exhausted. Women who had built impressive businesses and careers and still felt overwhelmed, disconnected, stretched too thin. Women who were doing everything they had been told to do and wondering why it still felt so hard.

Helping women build their businesses in a way that supports their lives has become the most meaningful work of my life, and not because I have all the answers, but because I understand the pattern. I know what it's like to perform your worth, how easy it is to mistake endurance for success, how difficult it can be to question a script you've been praised for following. And I also know what's possible when you're given (or forced into) the space to ask more meaningful questions.

When I think back to my childhood, to the hallway of achievements and the silent scoreboard I carried with me for years, I see it differently now. I understand why I chased gold stars so relentlessly. I understand why achievement felt synonymous with safety.

And I think back to that moment after I didn't make the rep soccer team, sitting on my bed while my mom tried to soften the disappointment. For a long time, I treated that part of myself like a problem. I thought life would be easier if I followed the rules more cleanly, if I didn't question so much, if I fit the mould more comfortably. But the "why" was never a flaw, it was the compass. It's what led me out of corporate and environments that harmed me. It's what allowed me to build a business differently, and now it's what allows me to help other women do the same.

I wasn't meant to perform success, I was meant to redefine it.

Today, success feels nothing like the version I grew up believing in. It doesn't live on a wall or require exhaustion. It doesn't ask me to disappear to prove my worth. **Success now feels like alignment and choice. Like a life I recognize when I'm living it.**

I'm building meaningful work without sacrificing myself. I'm able to be present for my family without guilt. And I'm able to trust my instincts instead of overriding them, knowing my worth is inherent, not earned from something I do.

I used to measure my life by how much I could carry. Now I measure it by how intentionally I live. **And that shift—from someone else's definition of success to my own—is the greatest freedom I've ever known.**

If you've looked at your life and thought, *This is supposed to be good, so why doesn't it feel good?* you may simply be ready to ask why.

Sometimes we don't choose the pause. Sometimes it's given to us: unexpectedly and inconveniently but exactly when we need it. And if you find yourself in that space, wondering what comes next, please remember that **you are allowed to build differently**

and redefine success. You are allowed to choose a life that fits you, even if it looks nothing like the one you were taught to want.

Success should feel like freedom, not endurance. And if it doesn't yet, it might just mean you're still becoming.

A NEW DEFINITION

The stories you just moved through weren't easy ones to tell. Dismantling what you've built, questioning what you've believed, disrupting the status quo, and choosing something different takes a particular kind of courage. If you felt something shift while reading, that's the resonance worth paying attention to.

Every woman in this book had a moment when the life she had built stopped fitting. Every one of them pulled the car over and looked at the destination on the map. And whether they charted a new path, or threw the map entirely out the window, they found that the thing waiting on the other side of letting go was more her than anything else she had been driving toward.

The stories in this book are done, but yours is just beginning. Look at your own dashboard. Where are you going and who set the destination? You might find yourself standing on the edge of a new definition.

As Georgia O'Keeffe said, "I always felt I walked on the edge of a knife. On this knife I might fall off on either side. But I'd walk it again. So what. So what if you do fall off? I'd rather be doing something I really wanted to do."

suc·cess /sək'ses/ — redefined

No longer a destination measured by titles, net worth, or the approval of others. **Success, in its truest form, is a living, evolving alignment between who you are, how you move through the world, and what you choose to honour along the way.** It is the courage to dismantle inherited definitions and architect your own. Not to create another box you must fit into, but to exist beyond the need for one.

For the entrepreneur, it is a business that breathes your values. For the thought leader, it is influence rooted in integrity. For the changemaker, it is a legacy that outlives the current moment. For every woman in these pages, it is choosing yourself, over and over again.

Success is not defined by what you achieve. It is the relationship you have with yourself while building it and the courage to keep rewriting what it actually means for you. This is success redefined, and it's a new era of empowerment!

THE MONARCH & CO.